An inspiring ennie Hudson
Taylor woul on, but in the
19th century was astonish-
ing. Often o ary literature
because of fo dson Taylor,
Jennie's story grace of God and
to a life lived for her Lord and Saviour. Her contribution to the
growth of the church in China was immense. More than a century after her death, her life still challenges us today to live fully, sacrificially, joyfully as contemporary disciples. Marion Osgood has captured the essence of it all beautifully.

Rose Dowsett, Missiologist, Author and Speaker

This fascinating and grippingly written biography of Jennie, Hudson Taylor's second wife, inspires and challenges. Such vibrant faith! Such willingness to suffer for Christ! Such passion for mission in China! Of course, nineteenth century mission approaches require considerable adaptation today, but let us join Jennie and her contemporaries in the thrill of worldwide mission! And may today's hundred million Christians in China, the fruit of their pioneering work, be freed to serve with us in God's international mission!

Martin Goldsmith, All Nations Christian College

Marion has unearthed the extraordinary story of Jennie, who although it's barely known, played a crucial part in the 19th century evangelisation of China. As second wife of the legendary Hudson Taylor she cheerfully defied the many restrictions that faced Victorian women and answered the missionary call. Jennie's unshakeable commitment to the Lord's work, her love of family and the Chinese people – especially the many children she educated and cared for – all combined to make her a true pioneer. Carefully sifting through CIM archives, including a wealth of the Taylors' correspondence, Marion has written a truly inspiring account that will encourage everyone who reads it.

Lyndon and Celia Bowring, CARE

Once you pick up this book it is difficult to put down! It is a very timely, well written biography of Jennie Taylor (née Faulding) – from curious child to second wife, and all the various stages in between. It is an amazing story of faithfulness – to God, Hudson, the CIM, her extended family, and all those whose lives entwined with hers. This includes a number of other significant Christian leaders and philanthropists, alive in those days of great blessing. Surely lives such as these should make us say, with Jennie Taylor, 'Who wouldn't want to be a missionary?'

Ruth Broomhall, great-grandniece of Hudson Taylor and Author

This long-awaited book brings Jennie Faulding Taylor out of the shadows, and pays tribute to her profound influence on Hudson Taylor and the China Inland Mission. Jennie was prominent in the second half of Hudson's life, as his darling wife, soul mate, prayer companion, and 'mother of the mission'. This book is a unique tapestry of their life journeys, interwoven with cultural nuances, spiritual encounters, intrigue, coherence and fascinating detail. A golden thread is Jennie's personal transformation from a happy privileged 19th century childhood in London to a magnanimous and indomitable pioneer missionary in China.

Dr Judy Lam, Spiritual Director,
Retreat Facilitator, and Researcher (Spirituality)

Most missionary biographies focus on famous men or a few pioneering single women. Marion Osgood gives us a compelling narrative of Jennie, Hudson Taylor's second wife, who worked both alongside him and independently in daring, dangerous incursions into inland China, where no Western woman had gone before. She learned multiple Chinese dialects, founded schools, worked with 'hidden' women and spent her life serving God sacrificially and with joy. Osgood has done us all, especially Christian women, a service in telling her story.

Veronica Zundel, Writer, Poet, and former
Chair of 'Men, Women and God'

While many would be familiar with the adventurous stories of Hudson Taylor and the China Inland Mission (CIM), few would know Jennie Faulding. As a young woman she was one of the first group of CIM missionaries who went to China in 1866. She approached life with a spirit of adventure, a strong sense of duty and an infectious enthusiasm. Going to China as a single woman, she would never have imagined that she would one day be facing a future wedded to the China Inland Mission. When she married Hudson Taylor in 1871 after his first wife, Maria, passed away, she would share concerns of finance, publicity, management, reputation, and a sense of responsibility for the lives of fellow missionaries in isolated and dangerous situations. One can feel the sights, smells and sounds of China. One cannot escape the agonizing pains of frequent deaths and separations, which permeate her life. Yet, we will be inspired by her ever-positive attitude and unwavering hope, full of gratitude to God despite the twists and turns in life. For those who seek to serve God's purpose for their lives, this book will not fail to inspire.

Rev Dr Patrick Fung, Global Ambassador,
OMF International

JENNIE HUDSON TAYLOR

An adventurous spirit, courageous faith, and a trailblazing call to China

Marion Osgood

Copyright © 2025 Marion Osgood

First published 2025 by Authentic Media Limited,
PO Box 6326, Bletchley, Milton Keynes, MK1 9GG.
authenticmedia.co.uk

The right of Marion Osgood to be identified as the Author of this Work
has been asserted in accordance with the
Copyright, Designs and Patents Act 1988.

All rights reserved.
No part of this publication may be reproduced, stored
in a retrieval system, or transmitted in any form or by any means,
electronic, mechanical, photocopying, recording or otherwise, without
the prior permission of the publisher or a licence permitting restricted
copying. In the UK such licences are issued by the Copyright Licensing
Agency, 5th Floor, Shackleton House, 4 Battle Bridge Lane, London SE1 2HX.

British Library Cataloguing in Publication Data
A catalogue record for this book is available from the British Library.
ISBN: 978-1-78893-341-4
978-1-78893-342-1 (e-book)

Cover design by Claire Marshall

This book is dedicated to the memory of
Dorothy Batten (6.9.1944–14.2.2023)
– close friend, great encourager, wise critic, and ideal companion on two visits to friends in China.

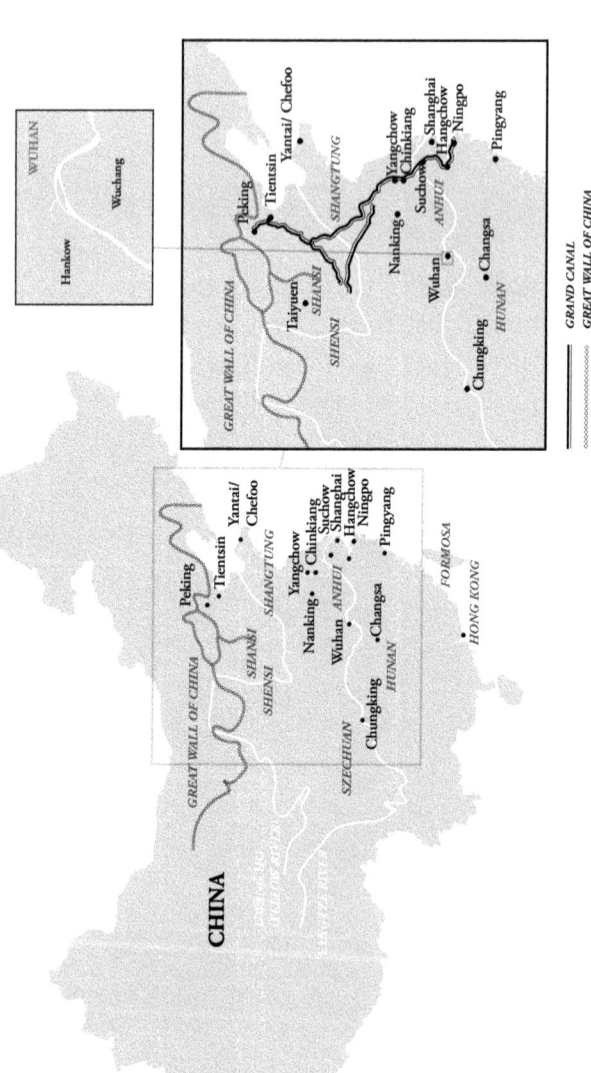

Hannah Li/OMF International (UK)

Contents

Acknowledgements xi
Foreword by Michele Guinness xiii

Introduction 1
1 Jane Elizabeth Faulding (1843) 5
2 Not a Moment to Lose (1853–62) 12
3 The Goings-on in Beaumont Street (1862–65) 20
4 Beginning to Catch the Vision (1864–65) 31
5 The Right Moment to Book the Passage
 (1865–66) 40
6 Securing All Moveable Objects (1866) 50
7 Picking Up the Hangchow Dialect (1866–67) 61
8 Loving Every Minute (1867–68) 73
9 Mentioned in the House of Commons
 (1868–70) 85
10 For Jennie it Would Be Life-Changing
 (1870–71) 96
11 Hudson Broached the Subject (1871–72) 106
12 Her Calling Was Now Very Different
 (1872–74) 119

13 The Mrs Taylor of the Party was Pregnant (1874–76)	132
14 Moving Forward at an Incredible Rate (1876–78)	144
15 The Dead and Dying Lay Everywhere (1878–79)	155
16 The Sanatorium of China (1879–81)	168
17 Who Will Look After My Boy? (1881–84)	180
18 Even Queen Victoria Received Her Copy (1885–89)	192
19 'I Do Not Get Sea-sick but Heart-sick' (1889–94)	207
20 The Penny Had Dropped at Last (1895–98)	222
21 A Mantle of Horror (1899–1903)	233
22 'We Match One Another Very Well' (1903–04)	247
Postscript	255
Appendix 1 Hudson Taylor's surviving children	257
Appendix 2 Summary of Jennie's six journeys to China	258
Bibliography	259

Acknowledgements

All direct quotations, unless otherwise stated in the text, are taken from the correspondence between Hudson and Jennie Taylor, or from other archival material, held in the China Inland Mission Archive in Special Collections at the School of Oriental and African Studies, University of London.

In addition to attending SOAS I have had in-person access to: London Metropolitan Archives; the Research Archive at Brunel University London; and the Angus Library and Archives, Regent's Park College, University of Oxford. I thank each of them for their help.

I have also made extensive use of the archives held at OMF International (UK) at Borough Green, Kent.

In addition to books listed in the bibliography, I have referred to China Inland Mission's *Occasional Papers*, *Monthly Notes*, and *China's Millions*, and the Australasian and the North American editions of *China's Millions*.

A note about spelling

Standardisation of spelling was virtually complete by the Victorian era, but not quite when it came to proper names. Patronymics were used extensively, but with no consistency of spelling. So where for instance Jennie's sister Ellen was known variously as Nellie or Nelly, I have chosen to use 'Nellie'. Even Hudson Taylor later in life started addressing Jennie as Jenny. I have maintained the use of 'Jennie'.

With Chinese geographical names I have used Wade-Giles spellings throughout, rather than Pinyin. This was in order to be consistent with the spellings used by the China Inland Mission at the time of the Taylors. Even within Wade-Giles, however, there is some degree of variation.

Thanks

Finally, I wish to thank my publishers, Authentic Media. I have appreciated so much their enthusiasm for my writing, and their encouragement and positivity throughout the publishing process.

Foreword

Long ago, I fell in love with the stories of pioneer missionary women. Living at a time when women rarely had access to the pulpit or any form of leadership in the church, they were such trailblazers, changing the world for me and for my daughter and granddaughter in their own inimitable way. But it came at huge cost – usually the loss of the presence and comfort of those they loved the most. We owe them a huge debt of gratitude.

Jennie Taylor, the exceptional second wife of one of the greatest missionary statesmen of all time, Hudson Taylor, founder and leader of the famous China Inland Mission, was such a woman. Without her he probably wouldn't have achieved half of all he did, yet little has been written about her life. In fact, google 'Hudson Taylor wife' and you will find most of the references are to Maria, his first wife. Ironic, since she died after only twelve years of marriage, while Jennie had thirty-three years of living and working alongside her beloved Hudson.

So, when I met Marion Osgood at the Christian Resources Together conference, I was thrilled to hear she had a passion to set the record straight, not least because I already knew of Jennie's great friendship with Geraldine Guinness, Hudson Taylor's daughter-in-law, and my husband's step-aunt, whose story I had told some years ago in a biography of the Guinness family.

Closely based on Jennie's letters home to the heartbroken parents she left behind when she set off for China, Marion has written a superbly researched, compelling account of Jennie's life. Like most of her female co-workers in the China Inland Mission, Jennie had to cope with many hair-raising adventures, difficulties, demands, sacrifices and challenges that would have floored most of us. But unlike her co-workers she not only continued her own innovative work, she then married the widowed founder and leader.

Like many great ground-breakers, Hudson Taylor was often exhausted, unwell, vulnerable, self-doubting, and susceptible to criticism, and he needed her support. Marion hasn't balked at telling the story honestly and as it was – the doubts, complexities, anxieties and disappointments that accompanied the many joys and achievements. And the pain of the long separations when neither wanted it but the work in China demanded it. 'An easy, non-self-denying life will never be one of power', Taylor once said. 'Fruit-bearing involves cross-bearing.' And they lived it.

Marion's ability to capture Jennie's wisdom, devotion, dedication and tireless self-sacrifice, torn as she was between her roles as teacher, initiator, wife, step-mother and mother left me breathless with admiration. It was Jennie who held out for women, married or unmarried, to be involved in the mission work in ways that had previously only been reserved for the men, and it had a profound influence on mission everywhere. The flame she lit in China still burns brightly there today, where many women are now pastors in the Chinese church.

I am so grateful for this engaging biography. It is a delightful and touching tribute to a very special woman. When I came to the end, it was with a heavy heart. I had come to know and love Jennie. I shall miss her and can't wait to meet her one of these days.

Michele Guinness
Author, journalist, Guinness family historian

Introduction

During my childhood I loved the missionary evenings that were held in our church; I thoroughly enjoyed the jerky film-strips with their uncoordinated soundtracks, telling us about faraway places. In my teens I devoured missionary biographies, and God used them to challenge and stir me. In reading stories from the China Inland Mission (CIM) I knew of 'Hudson Taylor's wife': her name was Maria, of course.

Now in my role as archivist for OMF International (UK), I have come to realise that that was not quite accurate. Maria died at a young age, and Hudson remarried. He was married to Jennie for almost three times as long. In discovering more, I also began to feel that Hudson and Maria's courtship and young love had been romanticised, whereas that with Jennie was portrayed as more prosaic ('no time for a honeymoon'). This was inaccurate also. Theirs was every bit the passionate love story.

Neither was there a book about her on the OMF shelves; she was just mentioned in that most demeaning of genres, the female compilation – where it is considered there is inadequate material for a full book.

Surely, I thought, if Jennie, with her small team of females, did indeed go hundreds of miles further inland from the coast of China than any other western woman had ever gone, she might be worthy of her own book.

It is difficult to overestimate just how remarkable Jennie Taylor was. Even the bravest most adventurous Victorian women generally found too many conventions prevented their escaping the narrow path mapped out for them.

The very few who managed it were in a class of bravery which, with safety of modern travel and healthcare, just does not exist nowadays.

Even within the church, with the awareness of the call of foreign mission, travelling abroad was still not thought possible for the majority of women or men. Each of the eleven adult women who set sail in 1866 as part of the first CIM party was literally one in a million. And of those, two were travelling with their husbands, one was meeting her fiancé, and one was under-age and returning to family. In all the many hundreds, if not thousands, who had already heard Hudson Taylor's call to China, only seven women were able at that point to respond freely. Jennie (as Miss Jane Faulding) was one of those women.

First there was the problem of women's financial and social dependence. Coupled with non-existent or rudimentary education, this effectively ruled out 80 per cent of the population within the working classes.

Another challenge was that of childbirth, the fear of which was very real. And class was no protection here, as the nation had been reminded in 1817, after the deaths of the much-loved Princess Charlotte and her baby, the heir to the British throne: even wealth, health, good nourishment and the best in so-called maternity care were no guarantee of survival.

For all women the natural excitement of pregnancy tended to give way to fear towards the end, and certainly for a first delivery. It was subconsciously accepted, and portrayed in contemporary literature, that women must suffer, and possibly die, in childbirth. Many male missionaries lost wives in childbirth in the early years of the Mission and, grief-stricken, nevertheless went on to marry once or even twice more.

Even complicated and restrictive female clothing made it laughable to visualise, let alone contemplate, travelling abroad under anything but the best possible 'Thomas Cook' conditions – and his tours had not yet reached China.

Jennie's background and her positive experience of family life, her naturally easy-going and adventurous personality, and above all her unshakeable commitment to obedience to the call of God, all combined to prepare her to be a true pioneer. She repeatedly found herself in situations requiring incredible initiative: within months of first arriving in China she was responsible for founding and running two schools. Yet throughout her life there were times when she was just 'holding the fort', looking after the family (including four stepchildren), and coping with piles of administration and correspondence, while her husband was the other side of the globe.

How she graciously managed the fine balance between responding to his sometimes distraught letters, and conveying his requests and updates to the Home Council, might be a new perspective for those already familiar with the life of Hudson Taylor.

So as I gradually encountered facts about Jennie's life, at the same time reading round the subject, I became increasingly convinced it was a gap in CIM/OMF history which perhaps I would be able to fill.

As I researched more deeply, particularly within Hudson and Jennie's voluminous correspondence, I felt I was becoming acquainted with her inner world. I have therefore written reflectively, largely from Jennie's own viewpoint, encountering alongside her, as it were, each stage of her life, while she at all times and most importantly walked closely with God.

Marion Osgood
December 2023

1

Jane Elizabeth Faulding (1843)

'Is she really?'

'Can it be true, what they've been saying?' The congregation leaned forward almost imperceptibly to gain a better view.

The bride was well wrapped against the winter cold – but yes, indeed it was so: those present in the ancient parish church of St Marylebone, London on that November morning of 1816 recognised the particular compassion of the bridegroom William Taylor in taking on responsibility for the widow Ann Collins and her unborn baby.

And sure enough, just three months later, on 24 February 1817, baby Hannah Harriet arrived. The new parents were slightly overawed to realise their little daughter would be one of the first to be christened in the just completed and rather grand edition of their historic church, boasting an enormous Greek-style portico and brilliant white façade, and dominating that section of Marylebone Road.

If Hannah Harriet Taylor had ever been apprised of her less-than-conventional parenting, it never worried her.

And she certainly had no notion of the future significance of her surname.

Meanwhile, almost a year later in far-off Yorkshire, another happy domestic scene had taken place. The biting east wind was whipping across the flat Humberside marshes, rattling the window panes throughout the little village of Swinefleet; but as Dr Francis Faulding took the short walk to the pharmacy to pick up his messages for the day, he had good reason not to notice the cold; his mind was on the fact his young wife, Mary, had just safely given birth to their second child – another lusty little boy.

Their eventual six children were all baptised at St Margaret's, as had been the custom from time immemorial – but Swinefleet awaited the completion of its first Primitive Methodist Chapel, opening in 1824. The journeys across the bleak Yorkshire landscape to hear John Wesley preach at Barnsley were well within living memory: many a heart had been kindled with a renewed love for God; many now longed that the fire would fall again. Primitive Methodism was a response to this longing, particularly for the working classes. In recent decades evangelical fervour had increasingly impressed itself on many of the new middle classes; now it was filtering down to the workers also.

Before universal primary education, those who remained illiterate had little to occupy their limited leisure hours beyond alcohol – unless they were caught up with the growing popularity of political agitation, or this, the even greater and more purposeful swell, of spiritual renewal; indeed, the latter acted as a brake on the worst excesses of the former. Chapel was becoming more popular than church, and in this at least, Swinefleet's labouring peat-cutters and their landowning masters were in agreement.

Francis and Mary called their newborn son William Joseph. But it was his older brother, Francis Hardey, who eventually followed in his father's footsteps; after a period of apprenticeship, he qualified as a surgeon and chemist, setting out from Liverpool as ship's surgeon. On arriving in Australia, he decided his fortunes would be well served by staying on, and he set up in Adelaide as a pharmacist. In time he developed his own manufacturing plant, later diversifying into veterinary medicines; the business of F.H. Faulding & Co. went from strength to strength. He became very wealthy, also taking up responsibilities as city councillor, and becoming something of a local dignitary.

But his reputation was always that of an active Christian and philanthropist. He remained within the Methodist church, supporting their missionary work. He also returned home frequently over the years, never forgetting his roots back in the Old Country. Married, but with no children of his own, he studied the progress of his younger brother William's family, taking particular interest in the daughters, those two brave nieces of his. Along with the rest of the family he watched in troubled amazement when first one then the other set off for the mission field. In regions more remote than anyone could ever have imagined they did indeed experience some periods of financial challenge; a remittance from their Uncle Francis was often incredibly timely – although the need had only ever been voiced to God alone.

William eventually demonstrated his own business acumen. By the time he was 20 he had moved to London, trading massive open skies for the smoke and noise of the city, in order to be apprenticed to a cabinet maker. And it was not long before he found his way to the parish church of St Marylebone, where the young Hannah Taylor caught his eye.

William Faulding married Hannah Taylor on 10 January 1843 at St Peter's, Saffron Hill in Holborn. Much to the young couple's delight they soon discovered a honeymoon baby was on the way, and Jane Elizabeth Faulding arrived on 6 October of the same year. Their first home was in Kingston, down the road into Surrey, and this was where Jane was born.

With growth in both household and bank balance, William and Hannah were soon looking for a larger and better placed home. They wished their children, most likely to be educated at home, to grow up enjoying the very best of whatever formative experiences this city and capital of Empire could offer. And, of course, everyone knew the air was sweeter to the west of London: the prevailing wind blew from the west, across Regent's Park's fragrant rose gardens, not from the City, the river, or the workaday East End.

They settled first in Edward Street, just off the Hampstead Road, and a short walk from the park. Here Jane's two brothers and her sister were born.

The family subsequently moved to a somewhat grander house on the Euston Road, with all the possibilities of modern communication both within London and without, seemingly right on its doorstep.

Nearby Euston Station had been the first of the great London railway termini to open, in 1837, followed by King's Cross, just a short drive further along the road, fifteen years later: trains were now speeding in from the north-west and

Jane Elizabeth Faulding (1843)

the north-east respectively, right into the heart of London. Next would be Brunel's Paddington Station, just along the road in the opposite direction, which would welcome his Great Western Railway into London in a year or so's time.

But things were not that straightforward. Fresh from the exhilaration of their journey, hundreds at a time were now pouring out of the trains onto the crowded station concourses; they hailed their hansom cabs, or climbed aboard the horse-buses if they were less well off. But how slow they found them now! Public transport had to compete with goods carts, road traffic had to contend with costermongers and pedestrians, and on wet days particularly, the quantities of horse manure were almost beyond endurance. Euston Road, the new super-highway, was grinding to a halt. And not to be outdone, the entrepreneurs of the Midland Railway were demanding their own route into the heart of the Metropolis; they planned to squeeze in yet another terminus, their very own St Pancras, one that would be the grandest of them all, between Euston and King's Cross. Something had to be done. The solution would be unbelievably radical.

The route of the first underground railway in the world was planned to follow the line of Euston Road, linking up all the termini, and finishing at Farringdon Station. It would be known as the Metropolitan Railway, and it would virtually run under the pavement right outside the Fauldings' front door! It would not be ready until 1863, but meanwhile colossal disruptive excavations began. A massive trench appeared, running the length of the road, steam shovels and cranes plied their noisy rhythm, and hordes of navvies shouted and swore above the din. When it was all over everyone breathed a sigh of relief, not least Isabella, the live-in maid, who could hardly remember a time when she was not cleaning mud off family shoes and clothing.

The route when complete was wildly popular, however. And above ground the only tell-tale sign was the occasional puff of steam issuing forth from an air vent – and the elegant Portland Square Underground Station, handy on their doorstep, and a massive compensation.

Mr and Mrs Faulding were increasingly of the nonconformist persuasion. As they moved into the more fashionable part of London, they discovered that many active Christians among their class were finding a freshness and reality in informal gatherings – such as the 'tea-meetings' at Tottenham. Many who gathered there were from successful business backgrounds, a number of Quakers among them. A new 'seriousness' was spreading, revival was in the air, and the fluidity in congregational loyalties no longer raised eyebrows.

Then suddenly towards the end of 1852, a new speaker appeared on the circuit: a somewhat intense but winsome northern lad was increasingly being invited to address the meetings. He was hardly a preacher, but his compelling message lifted their sights; it raised their awareness beyond their newly reawakened sense of God's presence in their lives, beyond even their conscience concerning the appalling needs of London's cholera-ravaged poor, to a new world-consciousness, of God's great love for the remotest peoples of the world.

There was something else about the 20-year-old also, which at first William Faulding could not put his finger on.

Then he realised: of course, like himself, he didn't have the smart London accent!

The Fauldings were as taken with him as everyone else. They invited the shy medical student, who seemed to be permanently hungry, back to dine with them at 11 Edward Street. Their children were asked to stand in line, to please shake the hand of Mr Taylor.

They soon learned he was a different kind of guest.

2

Not a Moment to Lose (1853–62)

Mr Taylor was making plans to go as a missionary to China. At first he disclosed little: small talk round the meal table was not within his range, and direct questions seemed to elicit abrupt scriptural replies. But when encouraged to warm to his theme it was a different matter entirely. He talked vividly and fondly of the people of China as if he had already been there – as if he already had a place for them in his affections. He had evidently been advised to bring his date of departure forward, and this settled entirely with his own desires. He was even abandoning his medical training; he talked as if there was not a moment to lose. The mutton grew cold on their plates as the family were carried along with the sense of urgency in his preparations.

They noted also his remarkable way with the children; he seemed to have respect for them and their opinions – so unusual for the men of his day. He chatted easily about his own two younger sisters, Amelia and Louisa, whom he was clearly missing. The Fauldings' eldest, 9-year-old Jane, now known as Jennie, would be just three years younger than

Louisa. And William, Jennie's younger brother, was 7; he was transfixed with the stories Mr Taylor told of his two pet squirrels – which had now been bequeathed one to each of his sisters. No one could keep pets like that in London. Neither were 2-year-old Ellen, now known as Nellie, nor baby Alfred neglected by this engaging young man, who offered to take his turn with a cuddle, as soon as there were any tears.

With the candid response of a child, Jennie allowed herself to be drawn out – by someone who was prepared to take her seriously. She loved listening to the descriptions of this distant land. The memories both of Mr Taylor himself, and the vivid pictures he painted, lodged themselves firmly in her heart.

Later in 1853 Mr Taylor did indeed leave for China. Many at the 'meetings' wondered if they would ever see him again. Was it really possible to risk so much, in a land so far away and so unknown, and return to tell the story? They continued to pray, as he had earnestly requested they should, but the prayers inevitably became less specific over the months. At first, they didn't write. After all, how did they even know he was alive? No one seemed to have thought of writing *poste-restante*, so that letters would be there to greet him on arrival. In time both Mr Taylor and his supporters came to regret this lack of forethought deeply.

Then suddenly, ten months or so after he had first set sail, letters started to come back. Not only had he arrived safely, he was full of praise to God for seeing him through many difficulties. In fact, a whole raft of things had gone wrong. The underlying burden of his letters, however, was that of deep contentment at knowing he was following

God's will, right where he was. To say he expressed a firm resolution to remain would be inaccurate: any alternative simply had not crossed his mind.

The Tottenham prayer meetings were launched afresh into enthusiastic and informed intercession. They heeded also his exhortations concerning their own spiritual lives – their need, as his, for a greater yet simpler trust in God.

They also began to write letters.

Jennie Faulding was educated at home alongside her brother William. This was at a time when a daughter's tutoring would often be sacrificed for the need for expensive private schooling for a son; but this was not the case in this family. In fact, it was Nellie who was eventually sent away to school.

Apart from lessons at home, exhibitions of all kinds, from the educational and 'improving' to the frivolous and entertaining, were increasingly accessible throughout London from around this time. Museums and art galleries were opening almost on their doorstep. The well-established London Zoo was just a healthy walk away, across Regent's Park. The South Kensington Museum, which eventually became the Science Museum, was opened in 1857. The pseudo-Greek temple housing the British Museum was already complete in Bloomsbury, and awaited anyone keen to see the cultural trophies of conquest and plunder. Academic curating was a developing skill at this time, and ensured exhibits were of maximum educational value; consciences were yet to be exercised as to whether the artefacts should be there in the first place.

A certain world-famous exhibition of another kind had settled in its final and prominent location just along the road from where the Fauldings lived; it was receiving even greater publicity due to the fact its creator, Madame Tussaud, had recently died.

The most famous exhibition of all was only intended to last for six months; the so-called Great Exhibition had stood in London's Hyde Park, incongruous, cathedral-like, and so vast it encompassed even the pre-existing elm trees. It had dazzled the world which came to pay homage, both to Britain's industrial prowess and to their own necessarily more modest contributions. And then it was dismantled – but in response to popular clamour and to everyone's delight it had been reconstructed on a high point in South London. And this time the surrounding gardens were designed to be as fantastic as the so-called 'Crystal Palace' itself: the fountains were the highest in the world, and what young visitor could resist life-size dinosaurs clambering out of what must surely be a primaeval 'swamp'.

For reading material, as childhood gave way to adolescence, the Fairy Tales of Grimm and of Andersen were replaced by the conscience-stirring novels of Dickens, Thackeray and Mrs Gaskell, all of which were beginning to find popular acclaim.

There were music and singing lessons, and poems to be learned by heart. The Romantic poetry of Wordsworth and Keats was currently fashionable. The compositions of the Poet Laureate, Tennyson, alongside the new skill of photographic journalism, were stimulating a more realistic attitude in the educated classes to events such as the recently fought Crimean War.

Early in 1857, a letter arrived from China addressed to Mr Faulding. Inwardly flushed with the thought that Mr Taylor had remembered him, he opened it eagerly.

The letter contained a specific request – there was something which perhaps only Mr Faulding could do. His cabinet-making turned 'machinist' business was successfully diversifying: the company was now manufacturing frames and frets for pianos, and additionally he was not short of business contacts. Would he be able to obtain a harmonium suitable for shipping? What was it about this young man that was so compelling? William Faulding was keen to do all he could to oblige. He later discovered that, after the lengthy process of fulfilling the request, then the transit to China, and finally its repair after the storms of passage, the harmonium formed a suitable surprise gift for Mr Taylor's new bride.

Later that same year Jennie's uncle Francis Faulding arrived for a prolonged visit from Australia. He was accompanied by his wife, Eliza, whom none of them had met. The family enjoyed showing them the sights of London – another excuse to indulge in the plethora of museums and art galleries. Francis and Eliza spent time in Yorkshire also, of course – but in all they were in and out of 340 Euston Road for an action-packed two years.

Then suddenly, in the November of 1860, news went round that Mr Taylor was back.

His health had suffered terribly: no longer the energetic young man, now he was stooped and slow. They heard it said he thought he might never return to China. But interest was piqued when they realised he had not returned alone! There by his side was his pregnant wife, exhausted after a terrible voyage, with a toddler, and a Chinese gentleman. On arrival Mr Taylor and the Chinese friend had both been seen wearing oriental attire; Mrs Taylor and the

Not a Moment to Lose (1853–62) 17

little girl were in hopelessly outmoded western dress. The Tottenham ladies wondered at the strange sight they must have made.

Mr Taylor's sister Amelia was now married and living in Westbourne Grove, Bayswater, a fashionable area of London not far from where the Fauldings lived. This was where the new arrivals stayed at first – and where they were restored to 'normal' dress, healthy diet, and acquaintance with new western plumbing. Amelia herself was enjoying a smooth second pregnancy; she did all she could for Maria Taylor, who was weary and barely coping with her third. Her baby was due in the spring, a month ahead of Amelia's.

Mr Taylor, true to his old form, was up and doing within a few days. Still far from well, he was nevertheless anxious to start the whirlwind of friendship renewal, and to introduce those who had loved, prayed for and missed him, to his delightful wife. William and Hannah Faulding were now within this widening circle; the warmth of exchanges concerning the harmonium meant Mr Taylor now referred to them as 'old friends'.

Then it was Christmas, and time for the Taylors plus their Chinese friend to journey to his parents' home in Barnsley, Yorkshire. They went by train, of course: before they had all stepped ashore at Gravesend, a port downriver from London, Wang Lae-djun, the Chinese member of the party, had had no notion even of what a train might be.

In the April of 1861 the Taylor family settled into a home of their own. Mr Taylor had realised he really needed to complete his surgery qualification, at the least, so they began renting a house in Beaumont Street round the corner from the London Hospital and just off the Whitechapel

Road; it was also a place where rents were more realistic than in the West End.

But first, on 3 April, baby Herbert was born in the reassuring surroundings of the Westbourne Grove home; with what some considered indecent haste, however, by the middle of the month Mrs Taylor was transplanted along with the rest of the family to the rather more make-do accommodation in Beaumont Street. She was clearly of similar mettle to her husband, with a tremendous capacity for work, even when still far from well. As well as medical studies, Mr Taylor was planning with Wang Lae-djun to translate hymns and books into Chinese, and to translate the Ningpo New Testament into a Romanised and more teachable script.

With Bible translating, letter-writing to China, developing contacts who were interested in the work, the needs of a growing family, and lectures at the hospital, the Taylors were soon committed to an exhausting round of multitasking. The Fauldings too got on with their lives, and apart from specific gatherings at which Mr Taylor had been invited to speak, they did not see so much of each other.

Then in the January of 1862, the Fauldings heard about plans for a regular weekly prayer meeting, to be held in the Taylors' Beaumont Street home. It would be specifically to pray for the spiritual needs of China.

For some time, Jennie had been developing a faith of her own, a relationship with her heavenly Father independent of her parents' instruction. At Regent's Park Baptist Chapel, a newly opened church round the corner from where the family lived, she was tuning in to the evangelistic and missionary-minded sermons of Dr Landels, the minister.

She had been baptised earlier in her teens, and at only 17 had joined the Ladies' Visiting Committee. There was a different side to her now besides the carefree disposition. She was still beholden to her parents, but she told them she would like to go to Mr Taylor's meeting.

3

The Goings-on in Beaumont Street (1862–65)

James Hudson Taylor was the archetypal young man in a hurry. He had set out for China when he was just 21 years old, not really expecting to return. He knew beyond a shadow of doubt that he was meant to be going – but in many ways the timing and manner were ill-advised.

He had linked up with the Chinese Evangelisation Society (CES), a newly assembled and well-meaning but as yet untested grouping. The roots of the CES went back to the brilliant but gullible Karl Gützlaff, the Prussian-born linguist, Bible translator and British diplomat in Hong Kong. Gützlaff's true missionary heart was sadly betrayed when he was seriously taken in by spurious converts; some of his naivety was carried through to this new organisation.

The CES were enthusiastic about young Taylor, and decided it would be good to get him out quickly. So, he went out with incomplete medical qualifications and with no theological training or denominational backing; he was the first candidate of an untried missionary society, and moreover he was unmarried; not necessarily all at once, but in time he came to regret each one of these deficiencies. There was clear reasoning behind this too-hasty departure, however: it was in order that the CES's new recruit would catch the crest of the Taiping revolutionary wave.

The Taipings were a pseudo-Christian sect turned army of freedom-fighters, first emerging in the 1830s. Their commitment to iconoclasm saw the destruction of pagan temples and numerous images. This, and their strict stand against opium, was beginning to have a cleansing effect across the region; it was generally thought they would usher in a new Christian era. Many missionaries were taken in for a while; it was a close call for even the most experienced, and the CES were not the only ones to be deceived.

But alas, the Taipings were given to horrific and increasing violence. They were sweeping across whole provinces, with the aim of establishing their capital in Nanking – and when Hudson Taylor first stepped ashore in Shanghai, the Taipings were there too. The Chinese Imperial army were fighting them in the streets; cannon fire was shaking the compound where Hudson spent his first night. It took someone of the calibre of General Gordon leading British and French troops alongside the Chinese, to finally defeat them in 1864. He was subsequently referred to by the British as Chinese Gordon (until eventually known to posterity as Gordon of Khartoum).

The missionary community in Shanghai became Hudson Taylor's base; they looked upon him charitably, but with his lack of qualifications, as somewhat of an oddity. As for Hudson, like many a raw missionary recruit he struggled with some erroneous 'observations': his staunch

Methodist background and youthful inexperience caused him to be silently critical of what he called 'worldliness' within the community. In all probability, Hudson had identified behaviours which had simply become a means of surviving emotionally in an alien environment. At the time of Hudson Taylor's arrival in China there were fewer than one hundred Protestant missionaries, not including wives, throughout the country. For the most part they were hard-working. That they were there at all, albeit spread across the five Treaty Ports in just four coastal provinces, was to them and to their supporters at home proof of the sustaining love of their almighty God.

Hudson Taylor's own single-minded commitment to his Godly calling was beyond reproach, however; within days of his arrival he had engaged a Mandarin language teacher, and was also accompanying the other missionaries on their evangelistic sorties beyond the confines of the city (allowed under Treaty Port law, within a thirty-mile limit). Even at this stage, with so much not having gone to plan, Hudson was at peace, and proving a delightful and selfless companion to others.

Hudson's relations with the CES soon began to deteriorate: they sent hopelessly inadequate financial provision, even for someone of Hudson's modest requirements. They then stunned him with their less than complimentary attitude towards the larger established missionary societies, who themselves sent realistic support to their own Shanghai missionaries – who were of course, somewhat ironically, showing great generosity to the hapless Hudson.

He could well bear his own sorrows, but it was the last straw when he learned the CES itself was borrowing money – a state he regarded as incompatible with biblical principles. Hudson Taylor was totally reconciled to being dependent on his good and faithful God alone, financially as well as in other ways: by 1857 he had resigned from the Chinese Evangelisation Society, forfeiting any residual support they might represent.

Meanwhile, wishing to minimise his embarrassing dependence on his new companions, Hudson had wasted no time in searching for somewhere of minimal rent in order to set up house on his own. He found a place in a poor and strife-ridden area, in need of much attention, but on the plus side with spare rooms for a future chapel or school – Hudson was totally committed to the long haul. He soon had it cleaned, and whitewashed inside and out, and he also began employing a cook.

Hudson Taylor was desperate to marry. In every way he longed for a life-partner, and in fact beyond the views of the time he considered a wife would be his equal alongside him in the work. It just seemed impossible that he would meet anyone where he was; there were at that time only about a dozen single western women in the whole of China. But wonderfully however, God had selected one of them especially for him.

Maria Dyer, orphaned daughter of missionaries to Penang, had been teaching in Ningpo, at the first Protestant missionary school for girls to be established in China. She and Hudson were married in January 1858, as soon as Maria was 21. This also happened to be the year of the significant Treaty of Tientsin, when nine more treaty ports were created, and journeys of more than twenty-four hours inland were allowed. (The original five Treaty Ports, Shanghai and

Ningpo among them, were part of the settlement following Great Britain's scandalous Opium Wars with China.)

The newlyweds were deliriously happy with each other, and full of gratitude to God for bringing them together. But following the honeymoon there was typhoid for both of them, then a stillbirth, then the arrival of baby Grace, and the death of Maria's sister, all in quick succession. By the spring of 1860, with neither of them fully recovered, they were being advised to come home. It was thought the fresh air and enforced rest of months on board ship might be restorative – in fact, with more illness, the beginnings of another pregnancy, and a bad-tempered captain, it was something of a nightmare.

Hudson Taylor was now a veteran of suffering and disasters of truly Pauline proportions. He and his wife appeared to have had more than their fair share of near-death experiences, even by this stage. Some of this at least would have to be put down to Hudson's naturally brave and pioneering spirit, and his sense of abandonment to what he saw as God's will – all of which could lead at times to a lack of caution. Added to this was his notorious corner-cutting economy.

But now back in London, for a while at least they appeared to be in safe and settled domesticity, albeit with a variety of fresh demands on their gifts and energies.

Having gained her parents' permission, Jennie eagerly anticipated the start of Mr and Mrs Taylor's Saturday afternoon prayer meetings for China.

The Taylors themselves, greatly recovered from their journeying ordeals, were now wondering if they might one day see China again after all: they were beginning to set their sights on a possible eventual return. Ironically it was partly the news that other missionaries were dying prematurely, or like them, had had to come home, which fired these thoughts. William and Hannah Faulding struggled with the recklessness of this idea; to Jennie, it was quite understandable – and beyond exciting.

A prayer meeting must surely be a safe enough option, however, so when the day came, her parents were happy to call for the hansom cab.

Well wrapped up against the damp winter air, Jennie spent the journey looking out on the bustling scenes which passed her by. As the hansom eventually took her out along the Whitechapel Road she suddenly caught sight of the imposing steps of the London Hospital. Mr Taylor had talked about his work there; she knew she must be getting near. But just after that, as the horse and cab clattered round the corner into tiny Beaumont Street, she felt a flutter of concern: it was not exactly the kind of area she was used to! Her mind went immediately to the time she first heard of the meetings: no, she had not made a mistake, from the outset she knew she was meant to have come. In contrast the ornamental Chinese scroll which caught her eye, on the front door by the bell-pull, struck a strangely reassuring note. Later she found out it said *Jehovah Jireh* ('God will provide'), in Chinese script. It had first been on the Taylors' front door in Ningpo.

The Taylors' commitment to the nation of China, and to raising greater prayerful interest in its salvation, now included a desire to send others out there; they realised, partly from Hudson's own experience, that a period of preparation and training would be a wise investment. The cheapest and simplest way to do this, at least while numbers were small, would be to use their own home. In fact, the prayer meeting was started at the point at which a Mr and Mrs Meadows had moved in to begin their training. For extra space the Taylors rented a room next door – a method of expansion which they used frequently from then on wherever they lived.

Even so, Jennie found the Taylor household cramped and overwhelming – and at first slightly intimidating; feeling lost among adults she didn't recognise, but who all seemed to have a job to do, she gravitated towards the baby and the toddler; they at least made Jennie feel at home.

Everyone settled eventually in a room heaving with books, maps and papers.

The fire in the grate was struggling against the winter cold, but as Mr Taylor started talking, now with the fervour of raw experience, Jennie soon forgot about the cold and the alien environment; catching the echo of his voice from her childhood, she was once more carried along on a wave of excitement, and the inescapable importance of what he was saying.

As the weeks went by Jennie lost the sense of alienation. Lulled by the comfort of Mr Taylor's soft Yorkshire vowels, so similar to her father's, she was also drawn more and more by her own personal commitment to pray for China. Far from it being a burden she enjoyed the sense of fellowship and shared goals which it seemed to engender.

She developed a habit of particularly watching Maria; she wondered how her unflustered manner coped with the constant demands and pressures, of home and family, and perhaps above all of the work for China; she started looking for ways to help. As spring turned to summer, Maria was tiring more easily. With generally lighter clothes being worn it didn't take Jennie's sharp eyes long to pick out that another little Taylor was on the way.

On 25 November 1862 a second son, Frederick Howard, was born in Beaumont Street. The family then disappeared off to Barnsley for another Christmas.

There was no doubt Jennie was growing fond of this unusual family. But as much as she was dreading their absence, she found the gap wasn't as big as anticipated; that autumn she was more than fully occupied with a new enterprise of her own.

Primary education that was both free and universal had always been dismissed by the government of Britain as an impossible dream. Now at last in the mid-nineteenth century, it was being seriously discussed, by government and academic circles alike. It would finally become a reality with the Elementary Education Act of 1870. Any form of higher education would remain the privilege of the upper classes alone, of course, for many years to come. But now slowly this group was beginning to include women.

It was partly a necessity. As primary schooling spread, so more female teachers were needed, and training and qualifications had to be standardised. In response to this growing need, in 1836 educationalist siblings Elizabeth and Charles Mayo had come to London, and established the prestigious Home and Colonial Training College – an Anglican foundation officially titled the Home and Colonial Infant School Society's Training School for Mistresses. It was housed in a rather grand building at the King's Cross end of

Grays Inn Road – part of Thomas Cubitt's new and impressive Bloomsbury development, the enterprise which was so transforming that area of London.

Elizabeth Mayo was the first woman in England to be employed in teacher training, pioneering the concept of infant school teaching as a discipline in its own right. Meanwhile in Switzerland her brother Charles had met and been influenced by the educational reformer Johann Pestalozzi – and an adapted form of the Pestalozzi system was used at the Home and Colonial College. Standing against the tide of rote learning, it introduced the first formal system of education for infants. Suited to children from even the poorest classes, it was well ahead of its time. The college was barely a mile from the Faulding home; Mr and Mrs Faulding decided this might be just the right place in which to invest in their elder daughter's future – they sent off for an application form. Having never applied for anything in her life before, Jennie approached the form cautiously. She need not have worried, however, as her home-spun but thorough education, coupled with her unassailably good upbringing was more than equal to the expectations.

A basic grounding in Bible knowledge, and in history and geography, was among the requirements. Her parents had to attest to her singing ability, and most importantly, her piety. Confirmation of this latter had to be given in writing from the applicant's vicar or minister. Proofs of smallpox vaccination and of debt-free status were required, and questions were also posed concerning any sign of the dreaded 'consumption' within the wider family. Finally, a short piece of writing was requested as demonstration of basic literacy, accompanied by samples of the candidate's sewing and darning ability.

Jennie's application was successful. Her father having paid her board and lodging fees (all else being paid for by the government) she commenced her two-year training.

The premises actually included its own 'model' infants' school, with 300 pupils, and fifty teachers in training. On the ground floor there were 'practice' classrooms, and the real thing. There was a central courtyard, naturally forming the playground, and ranged around this on upper floors were the usual student facilities and accommodation. Each floor was appointed with the latest in indoor plumbing – an essential requirement when catering for young ladies drawn largely from the middle and upper classes.

The stated aim of the college was 'for the Improvement and Extension of the Infant School System and the Education of Teachers at Home and Abroad'. It followed that any graduate, as well as being well-equipped, would be seen as influential and definitely *avant-garde*. Many would become leading educationalists and philanthropists, fulfilling pioneering roles at home and abroad. And to add to the college's undoubted kudos, Queen Victoria herself was patron.

The 'colonial' aspect was due to the fact that a handful of the students came from the colonies of the time. Mission work, particularly in India, and particularly that carried out by the Church Missionary Society in Bengal, was elevating the standard of education in the area. There was thus a need for trained teachers, and as well as the expectation that some students would eventually go as missionaries, a steady trickle of the most suitable young women from India were sponsored to come to London to be trained. This was a fascinating link for Jennie; mesmerised by stories from their colourful backgrounds, she took stock of the fact that India, as well as China, was full of people loved by God.

But she soon found she had another distraction.

Emily Blatchley, a fellow student, was of similar age to Jennie. She and Jennie took to each other almost straight away; immediately companionable in both work and relaxation, they offered a mutual well of encouragement whenever classroom work became tiresome, or study perplexing. And Jennie soon realised her new soul-mate had longings and sensitivities much like her own: it was only a matter of time before Emily became curious as to the goings-on in Beaumont Street – soon she was attending the purposeful gatherings also.

Emily was already an orphan; she had been lodging with her brother in Carnaby Street, an insignificant little lane behind the glamorous shops of Regent Street. There was, of course, always a warm welcome for her within the doors of the Faulding household, and away from college life the girls spent many happy hours together. This included attendance with Jennie's family at Regent's Park Chapel, where Mr Faulding was now one of the elders; he was also on the Foreign Missionary Society Committee.

When it was time to graduate, in 1865, Emily, in need of some income, was successful in gaining a position as a school teacher straight away. Jennie's future remained uncertain. But one thing was definite: they had both received the privileged grounding that would equip them supremely for whatever plans God was going to reveal.

4

Beginning to Catch the Vision
(1864–65)

The Fauldings and others on the 'Tottenham circuit' were excited. London was currently a place of extraordinary spiritual blessing: congregations were growing, across all denominations; new missions were being founded, for work at home and abroad; the Methodist loss, of street preachers William and Catherine Booth, was about to become the world's great gain; and the soon-to-be-famous Charles Spurgeon was holding 5,000 spellbound every Sunday in his brand new Baptist 'Tabernacle' in Southwark. For those of an Anglican persuasion, William Pennefather the popular vicar of Christchurch, Barnet, was holding regular conferences on 'holiness', the current watchword representing a new seriousness of devotion to Godly lifestyle and obedience. When the Pennefathers left Barnet, for William to take up a living at St Jude's, Islington, the blessing continued, and his popular conventions became the Mildmay Conferences, soon to be held in a new 3,000-seater hall. (These eventually metamorphosed into the annual Keswick Convention, still going strong 150 years later.)

But best of all for his increasing band of supporters, Tottenham's Mr Taylor seemed to be at the heart of things, with invitations to preach in churches across the denominational board. His close and enduring relationship with both the Spurgeons and the Pennefathers dated from this time.

Hudson Taylor however was holding lightly to all his denominational attachments – and with good reason.

The Saturday gatherings were now left in no doubt that the Taylors' hearts were set on an eventual return to China. But week by week they were updated on the quandary: with which organisation or missionary society should they go? The Church Missionary Society would be keen to see him ordained – but Hudson Taylor was no 'churchman'; alternatively, there was the Baptist Missionary Society. With his Methodist background, and current involvement with the Brethren, he must keep his options open. An additional complication was that more and more the Taylors were feeling called to the interior of China – and for the time being, the established missionary societies were content to remain within the Treaty Ports.

But meanwhile those attending the prayer meetings were not allowed to forget the basic, undiluted message: China needed to hear of God's great salvation, and a mighty army of workers was needed to take the good news.

The Taylors continued to enjoy the Fauldings' hospitality, spending time with them at 340 Euston Road; for their part the Fauldings pushed to the back of their minds the fact that Mr Taylor might actually be crazy enough to take his young family back to China. On the positive side, they were aware of the sense of purpose his message was bringing into their elder daughter's life; Mr Faulding even

Beginning to Catch the Vision (1864–65)

occasionally accompanied her to Beaumont Street. They supported the Taylors with financial gifts; they were beginning to catch the vision.

In the summer of 1864, it was at last time for Hudson Taylor's faithful friend Lae-djun to return to China. He had given sterling service in almost every area, not only in the translation work for which he had primarily accompanied them. He had gained a place in many hearts, and a significant send-off was planned from Gravesend – and Jennie wanted to go.

When the day came, she joined with the rest of the farewell party boarding the train at the new Charing Cross Station. They got off at Gravesend, and walked out along the pier; then just what she had secretly been hoping – they were allowed on board Lae-djun's ship! Trunks and tea chests, crates and barrels, coils of the thickest rope she had ever seen . . . even the smells were transporting her imagination far away from Britain's grey shores. There were even cages of live animals! She did not dwell on what their fate might be – but decided travelling to China must be just the most wonderful adventure. Others were bound for China on the same ship, so there was in the end quite a crowd to join together in prayer, and the singing of a hymn, before farewells were finally said.

Meanwhile, with candidates for China still needing training, Beaumont Street was bursting at the seams; in the October the Taylor family moved to a more spacious dwelling in Coborn Street, another turning off the Mile End Road; beyond the Regent's Canal and further from the City, it would be a slightly quieter area. The prayer meeting moved too, of course: with news that Mr and

Mrs Meadows had arrived safely in China, things were gaining momentum.

And in December, although still studying, Jennie again offered Maria some help. A fourth baby, Samuel, had arrived the previous summer, and Maria was far from well. With so much serious interest in China, preparations seemed to be constant. A few candidates were committed to going with other agencies, but were nevertheless in training with the Taylors. Apart from anything else, they would all need kit. There must be plenty of sewing she could help with, Jennie suggested to Maria in a letter. She let slip also, that she, Jennie, was now beginning to cherish hopes that one day she too might be considered worthy to set sail for China.

This could be a bombshell for the Fauldings! Naturally Jennie broached the subject with them. As Godly people they decided they would not be closed to the idea, but coped for the time being by pushing it into the future. Jennie, however, with the usual impatience of youth, discovered as she talked to them that her commitment to China was stronger than she had thought.

But they were prepared to keep the discussion open, even suggesting their daughter have a conversation with the minister of their church. Perhaps he might point her in the direction of some safer, home-based work. In Dr Landels, Jennie was relieved to find a wise counsellor. He recognised her turmoil, in a deepening commitment to going to China, alongside the potential grief at the thought of upsetting particularly her mother; on the other hand, he understood the genuine parental concern. They continued to pray together about it – and settled on a 'yes' for two years' time! This for Jennie was a wonderful compromise – apart from the thought that the two years' wait might actually be good for her, it gave her just the excuse she needed to start learning Mandarin.

Meanwhile her friend Emily's desires were moving in a similar direction – she too was becoming burdened with the insistent call of China's 'lost' millions: learning Mandarin together became another fun activity for their limited spare time.

By the June of that year, 1865, it was becoming obvious to Jennie and others that all was not well with Mr Taylor. Was he not coping with the pressure of all his responsibilities? Certainly progress was good, interest was growing, candidates being prepared, and money being donated – although nowhere near enough. Was that the problem? Or was leadership weighing too heavily?

His passion for China was as great as ever. He had recently started work on a small book: called *China: Its Spiritual Need and Claims*, its pages throbbed with his heartbeat for the vast land of China and its people. When completed, its 120 pages read as one long letter: unfettered by chapter breaks or sub-headings, Taylor poured forth his objective and compelling mathematical arguments for the urgency of the task in hand. His numerical calculations, of exactly how many workers would be needed to reach the population of each province, were thoroughly researched – although they did not seem to allow for the fact that Chinese converts would themselves multiply. Quotations were included from his own journal and that of others, and it was this personal nature of his appeal, with names, dates and recent events all mentioned, which as much as anything gripped Jennie's attention. Along with everyone else in Hudson Taylor's growing circle, she obtained her copy and devoured it eagerly.

Then having gleaned all she could from her own copy, and drawn by her own commitment to the message, she quickly volunteered to publicise it, and to encourage others to do the same.

Yet Hudson Taylor's usual joy in the Lord was not so evident at the moment. Ironically, the sense of revival in London congregations was adding to his problem – how could these dear people, many of whom supported him, sing so volubly about the gospel spreading round the globe – if they were not prepared to take part in the spreading? His old spiritual intensity seemed to be threatening a comeback.

He seemed, on the one hand, to be increasingly burdened for the inland Chinese: he was becoming so overwhelmed he appeared to be making himself ill; on the other hand, he did not seem able to grasp the nettle of asking for more workers. Perhaps it was not his responsibility. Certainly, those closest to him wished a solution could be found rapidly.

But things were coming to a head; a friend invited him to take a weekend off and go to stay with him in Brighton.

As well as engaging in intense conversations, and attending church, he spent much time alone, walking along the beach, and talking to his heavenly Father. He threw stones in the sea, and kicked the sand where the tide had pulled out. Then suddenly it came to him – a revelation from God of divine equipping – to invite workers to form a team under his leadership. Further, he realised for a new work inland he needed a new agency, one that was free of any denominational tie. It should be called the China Inland Mission. He grasped fully what he had really always known, that the God who had looked after him would be utterly trustworthy in enabling him to lead and inspire others.

Beginning to Catch the Vision (1864–65)

Hudson Taylor came back a new man!

Back in the prayer gathering in Coborn Street, everyone noticed the difference. His anguish had clearly gone, and a look of quiet joy once again shone out of his eyes. Compared with the months of desultory effort, battling with his own doubts, how much easier it was now to inspire others. It was as if they had been waiting for him to grasp what they had recognised all along.

This was the summer of Jennie's and Emily's graduation. Now free of study, one of the first things they were looking forward to would be Mr Pennefather's huge Mildmay Conference, to be held in the October. Hudson Taylor's new 'pamphlet', as he called it, sold well there – so much so, it was reprinted almost straight away.

The reprint carried details of the newly created China Inland Mission, including the bank account, opened in that name the day Mr Taylor had returned from Brighton. A friend had given a small printing press to the Taylors; with Emily settling into her new school-mistress position, it did not take Jennie long to find her own latest project: always keen to acquire a new skill, she had soon mastered this efficient piece of technology. She was spending even more time in Coborn Street, first proof-reading the new edition, then printing it.

Meanwhile the Fauldings could see what was happening – and for them the challenge was almost overwhelming. Mrs Faulding, particularly, struggled with defensive thoughts. Could their lot be harder than most? After all, there was no Mr or Mrs Blatchley to worry about Emily's similar obsession with the other side of the globe; Maria Taylor too had no parents to be concerned. Others among the single women who were now openly talking of going to China were either older, or were planning to rejoin family or fiancé there. Jennie's parents felt keenly the impending threat of the sharp knife of separation from their daughter.

Jennie herself was of an uncomplicated disposition. She approached life with a spirit of adventure, and a great sense of fun. Together with all who have youth and health on their side, she had a sense of inviolability, rather than of being called to reckless sacrifice. But there was a strong sense of duty, and increasingly an awareness of the call of God on her life. She felt an overwhelming need to know that whatever she were to do, her life must count for God. And she now knew she was called to China.

By now Jennie had no qualms about the atmosphere of the Taylor home: although purposeful chaos seemed to reign, she was very much a part. She was bemused by the fact that she could be comfortable both in her parents' warmly cushioned and well-ordered environment, and in this humbler abode. Here it seemed not an ornament, not a picture on the wall, but it was there to serve a higher purpose, not merely that of decoration. Even the unmatched crockery and patched upholstery seemed marshalled for the cause.

She was now meeting many arriving from different parts of the country, moving into one or other of the houses Mr Taylor rented in Coborn Street, to begin their 'missionary training'. Young, fresh-faced Tom Barnardo from Dublin was one, single-hearted for the work which was calling him to China. But it was finding himself allocated to street work for his practical experience which did for him. In the haunted look in the sunken eyes of London's East End waifs he found his true destiny. He had come oh-so-close to being part of the early China Inland Mission story.

It was towards the end of 1865 that Hudson Taylor made what appeared to be his first and perhaps only excursion into secular acclaim: he successfully applied to become a Fellow of the Royal Geographical Society. In recent months he had found the archives at the RGS to have been helpful in his detailed writing and his increasingly well-informed motivational speaking on China. Now some of his influential and upper-class London friends were encouraging him to apply for Fellowship, and three of them acted as his sponsors. When news came through of his acceptance in the November, Hudson Taylor was ridiculously busy; it was left to his band of comparatively more 'ordinary' friends to celebrate this unheard-of achievement, on behalf of their Mr Taylor. With an annual subscription from then on, he was able to use FRGS after his name. Never a fully qualified 'doctor', he was happy to place it alongside his MRCS, his surgical qualification. The two sets of initials appeared after his name on many of the publications and periodicals written or edited by him, until well into the 1890s.

What a year 1865 had been, for Jennie, for her new CIM friends . . . and for some of the greatest Christian activists the world had ever seen. Within days of Hudson Taylor's life-changing Brighton beach experience, the Booths were founding their work, later to be known as the Salvation Army, in a tent mission barely a stone's throw from Coborn Street; Lord Shaftesbury's parliamentary Act of the year before was just beginning to change the lives of little boy chimney sweeps, and the following year the soon-to-be-famous Dr Barnardo opened his first children's home.

5

The Right Moment to Book the Passage (1865–66)

On Brighton beach, after his moment of revelation, Hudson Taylor had prayed for twenty-four men and women of the right calibre to take to China. He was now assembling that team. Jennie and Emily were wondering if they might possibly be included in this first draught.

Hudson had a radical approach to the role of women: he saw them not 'just' as wives of missionaries, but as missionaries in their own right. (The pattern in other missions was that the man, either ordained or medically qualified, would be the actual missionary, the wife being merely in a supportive role.) But even further, Hudson considered there was a need for single women. Unless women were seen to be as vital as men in the work, how would the Chinese women ever be reached with the gospel?

He was ahead of his time, but nevertheless beginning to carry his supporters along with these radical ideas – including among the increasing number of his wealthy, titled and socially influential friends.

Naturally, his recruits would have to be both spiritually and physically fit for the task, and prepared to submit to the Taylors as their leaders. As trainees moved into Coborn Street, there began a process both of rigorous training, and possible elimination.

Jennie and Emily's relationship with the Taylors was different, however. From the start they were looked upon by the Taylors more as younger members of their family. William and Hannah Faulding (with whom Emily was currently lodging and attending church) saw the relationship in this way also; in recognition of the fact that the fateful day of leaving was looking increasingly likely, they had asked the Taylors specifically to 'look after' Jennie. They wanted to know they (the Taylors) would always provide a home for their daughter.

As for the two girls themselves, they saw their role as more of helping than training. They both loved and respected the Taylors, so were sensitive to their needs.

Maria, pregnant once more, and once more far from well, was struggling with all the demands of the household, including her husband's considerable secretarial requirements. Emily stepped forward to help, and in fact proved so useful she secured a release from her teaching contract, and moved in with the Taylors. At first, she was governess to the three eldest children – but as Maria grew worse more radical solutions were required: the three lively little charges were sent up to stay with Hudson's parents in Barnsley. Jennie offered to look after 18-month-old Samuel, and both girls shared the almost overwhelming administrative demands of the new Mission. Maria, now giving her husband cause for even greater concern, possibly over developing TB, was taken to stay with their close friends the Bergers, in their beautiful and expansive home in the Sussex countryside.

Maria eventually survived the precipitate and dangerous delivery – but the baby girl did not. All those who cared deeply for the Taylors were heartbroken; this included Jennie of course, who was nevertheless surprised and touched that the baby's name, for her very short life, was Jane.

In the early months of 1866, it looked as if Hudson Taylor might have his definitive team. If maritime weather conditions were to be taken into consideration, they must leave no later than the end of May. Maria was still weak, but a sea voyage was surely all she needed for a return to health.

Jennie knew she was now included in the party. She moved into Coborn Street, as much as anything to maximise her invaluable support role. Her parents, reassured that she would always be regarded as a member of the Taylor family, and having exacted a promise that she would return after five years, were now totally supportive. To spend time with their daughter they visited the Taylors; this seemed to work better than expecting her to take time off to visit them. Coborn Street was looking more and more like a packing station for the Far East, with trunks and crates taking up more and more room in the three neighbouring houses; the bustle and clutter were all fun to Jennie's younger sister, Nellie, who often accompanied her parents. If it flashed across the Fauldings' minds that there might be a risk of a similar destiny attracting another of their children . . . they dismissed it rapidly.

Hudson Taylor was already well known at Regent's Park Chapel, having been invited to preach on several occasions. Dr Landels regularly attracted a congregation of almost two thousand, yet he had time for individuals also: there was a moving farewell service held for Jennie and Emily.

Jennie, always on the lookout for ways to both contribute to preparations and publicise the cause, galvanised some of the ladies of the chapel into action: forty of them 'signed up' to sew kit for the departing missionaries. Being a well-to-do congregation, many of them owned the new must-have domestic sewing machine.

Another of Hudson Taylor's radical tenets of foreign mission was that intellectual qualities were not always essential; on the contrary, a balanced team would consist of those good with their hands and experienced in a trade, as well as those with the kind of minds that could handle Bible translation or literacy work.

Jennie had to grow comfortable with this. She had never rubbed shoulders before with anyone, men particularly, from the working classes. She was now sitting alongside them in prayer meetings and at mealtimes; the nuances of her own upbringing just were not there! Her faith in Hudson Taylor was absolute, however; she trusted his reasoning, and soon found trustworthiness in the men concerned also. This was just as well; when it occurred to her they might quite genuinely wonder whom they would eventually marry – well, that did not bear thinking about!

In the end all the men who were included in the team were craftsmen rather than men of letters: there were two carpenters, two blacksmiths, a gardener and a stonemason.

Hudson Taylor decided that a regular update should be provided for their supporters, and others who might be interested. Called the *Occasional Paper*, the first one came out at the beginning of 1866. It was a report on plans so far, as well as a painstaking account of the current and most encouraging financial position. A summary of Taylor's 'missionary mathematics' was also included, carried forward from his first publication. There were clear indications of the fact William Berger was to be the one to hold the line at home; his name appeared as auditor of the accounts, and future correspondence was all to be addressed to him: their relaxed and comfortable country residence would soon become the busy CIM home base.

In spite of the seriousness, not to say risk, of the planned enterprise, an unavoidable air of excitement was building. Jennie was naturally a party to this, but she was also a hard worker, and only too aware of how much was still to be done. She noticed that even Mr Taylor's vast capacity for work was currently stretched to the limit. When he first went to China, he took responsibility for all his own preparations; now he seemed to struggle with allowing others to pick up on responsibilities in the same way – particularly in relation to their own kit and finance. The Coborn Street households prayed and worked hard; they were taught that God alone was their ultimate provider, but there was an ever-present undercurrent of Hudson Taylor's sense of personal responsibility. Added to this was his punishing speaking schedule, which seemed to demand he travel to opposite ends of the country's railway networks, sometimes on consecutive evenings. With Maria still away in the country, Emily and Jennie were often left organising day-to-day affairs.

And all the while, Mr Taylor was on the lookout for the right moment to book the passage.

There was no great expectation that the team, now consisting of about twenty, would all travel together – apart from the fact that Jennie and Emily were guaranteed to travel with the Taylors; the even younger Mary Bausum, returning to her family in China, and Mary Bell, the children's nurse, were in the same category. Separate passages might have to be booked for everyone else. But Hudson and Maria were aware of the undoubted advantages of ongoing team-building and training, should a ship big enough to take them all just happen to become available.

Whatever the eventual number of separate passages, it was certain they would not be on one of the new-fangled steam ships everyone was talking about; they were still a comparatively rare sight, and still expensive. Rather, this was the age of the 'clipper', the magnificent iron-framed sailing ships that were now so fast they were even having races, for the prestigious accolade of being first to arrive back with their cargo of China tea.

So, it was to be expected that clothes would easily become tar-stained during a sea voyage aboard a wooden, albeit iron-framed, sailing ship. For this reason, on top of everything else, Jennie was collecting second-hand clothing for the voyage.

Meanwhile Hudson Taylor was in frequent touch with a shipping agency. Trusting he would have the money for the deposit, he was planning to book the passages for the end of May.

But instead, the shipping agency contacted him.

A ship which might meet his criteria had just come in to the East India Docks. The *Lammermuir*, as it was called, was big enough to take the whole team, and would be ready to sail again by the end of May. Would he care to inspect it?

Hudson Taylor lost no time in viewing the vessel, and placing the required deposit. With a crew of thirty-five, they would be the only passengers.

Now there was not a moment to lose – they were sailing in three weeks!

Prayer cards with a list of the names of the party were hurriedly run off on the Mission's home printer. Hundreds of these were distributed at the final round of farewell meetings; the little wooden China Inland Mission money boxes were also much in demand. Many of the practical arrangements fell to Jennie, with Emily maintaining a tireless correspondence with Mr Taylor, enabling him to keep his finger firmly on the pulse of preparations, even when in a different part of the country.

Photography had to be a priority, in order to provide tangible mementos, and to maintain that essential prayerful interest after they had departed. As advertised in the *Occasional Paper*, an individual portrait of any member of the team could be purchased, at a modest price. And a group photo of the team was to be taken in the back garden of one of the Coborn Street properties. This took some organising: who should sit, who should stand? And who must help to hold the attention of four lively children, until everyone was ready? Eventually all were assembled on the back terrace, and there were several good 'takes', until the children's patience finally ran out. In addition to the six Taylors, and Jennie, Emily and the two Marys, there were the six men, one of whom was accompanied by his wife, and five other women. (Of these five, three had some Bible training, and one was a governess.) So, the final tally, with the children, was twenty-two. This comprised what became known as the *Lammermuir* party.

Never before had such a party been assembled, for such a purpose; it was experimental in size, and in its mix of gender, class and denominational loyalties; in human terms it was financially fragile, indeed many considered the whole enterprise breathtakingly audacious. All the party were unshakeable in their trust in God, however; Jennie, excited about every aspect save that of seeing her mother frequently in tears, was sure they were all going to get on splendidly.

Preparation and packing gathered pace; Victorian outfitting and underwear was complex – in order that no item be forgotten, a detailed tally was kept for each person, in the precise size required. Others, chiefly Jennie and Emily, did the shopping, but as in all things Hudson Taylor took close interest and ultimate responsibility. Uniformity was considered advisable, as there would be a risk of gross disparity if each person were allowed to choose their own kit.

Furniture and furnishings were needed for the cabins. In fact, all the necessities for life on board, and for much of their future life in China, had to be assembled. All writing and study materials, sewing and mending equipment, printing presses, workmen's tools, medical and toiletry requirements, all bedding, including mosquito nets – the list went on. When once they were given access to the ship, with little more than a week to go, twenty or thirty trunks or packing cases, or small items of furniture, were taken on board every single day. Food was the only thing they did not have to consider, as that was fully covered in the cost of the passage.

Everyone was allocated their cabin, and could plan the necessary furnishing ahead of departure. Jennie became quite used to the sight of her cabin (which she would be sharing with young Mary Bausum). Emily was in the cabin next door, with little Grace Taylor.

Mr Faulding gave up time to come on board, and to make Jennie's cabin as homely as possible, with well-secured bookshelves and a writing desk. She was delighted with the results: how could she feel anything but entirely safe and comfortable within this cosy and attractive new home?

In the final two or three days, and with the rent on the Taylors' properties terminated, the party dispersed either to their own homes, or as guests with others. Almost the last item to leave Coborn Street was the Taylors' treasured harmonium. After the final hymn at their final gathering, the 'Faulding' harmonium was cased up and transported onto the *Lammermuir*, to be installed centre stage in the stern cabin, ready to make its second journey to China.

The morning of Saturday 26 May 1866 dawned bright and sunny. The East India Docks were as noisy and busy as ever; this was where the tea clippers always docked, and where their precious cargo was unloaded. Here the *Lammermuir* party converged on the dockside, together with a considerable number of friends, relatives and supporters, assembling to see them off. William, the older of Jennie's two brothers, was there with his parents, looking forward to his first experience of stepping on board a ship. As well as his parents, Willie proved in time to be a good if less frequent letter-writer. William and Mary Berger, from now on the key couple in the home support team, came on board also; not all the *Lammermuir* party knew just how vital they were to the work, or to the lives of the Taylors.

Jennie was trying to savour every minute – but with the general atmosphere of chaos, last minute things to be thought of and the farewell party tripping over multiple packing cases still waiting to be sorted or stowed, the final hours sped past. At least there was little time for sadness. And all the while the bemused crew were standing by, waiting to see what they had let themselves in for.

There were tearful prayers, and the singing of a hymn (much to the consternation of some of the crew), then just before the ropes were finally released, most of the farewell party returned back down the gangplank and onto the dockside. Just a handful, including Mr Faulding, had arranged to stay on the ship until Gravesend. One of the dockland's new steam tugs began to tow the *Lammermuir* very slowly towards the lock gates and out into the Thames. None of this was easy for Hannah Faulding. Was this the moment when she was about to give up her elder daughter forever?

6

Securing All Moveable Objects (1866)

The friendship of Mr and Mrs Berger had become increasingly important to Hudson and Maria in the years leading up to their departure. A generation older than the Taylors, it was not just their wisdom and experience which were valued; they were spiritually attuned also. The Bergers were heart and soul for God's work in China. They were wealthy too, as it happened, and unstinting in their financial support. Everyone knew of the highly successful Berger's Starch Works in the East End, and of Berger Hall, the chapel nearby for the workers; Mr Taylor had often spoken at Berger Hall.

One of Mr Berger's first tasks, after bidding farewell to the *Lammermuir*, was to publish the second *Occasional Paper*. He reproduced Hudson Taylor's pre-prepared letter, then added a letter of his own; addressing his readers as from Saint Hill, his country home near East Grinstead in Sussex, he was effectively now the Mission's first home director. In the letter he took the opportunity to vouch for Hudson Taylor's transparent calculations when it came to money: only monies designated specifically for the Taylors would be so used; there was absolutely no risk of the mixing of personal and communal finances. Their trust in each other's dealings was clear for all to see.

There was then a long letter and report from Mr Meadows in Ningpo. (He had sadly already been widowed, but was awaiting his new fiancée on board the *Lammermuir*.) This was followed by the financial report.

At Gravesend, where most who were not passengers left the ship, Tom Barnardo greeted them on the dockside with some wine and extra provisions! Mr Faulding, in fact, remained on board until finally leaving with the river pilot at Deal on the Kent coast; here another pilot came on board to negotiate the notorious Goodwin Sands, leaving them at Dungeness – where the last mail, twenty-four items, was taken ashore. It was only after watching her father finally disappear that Jennie gave in to her emotions, allowing herself at last to retire sobbing to her cabin.

Everyone was seasick to some extent as, still in sight of the English coast, they anchored in choppy waters waiting for a favourable wind. Jennie and Mr Taylor were least affected, and after this, with most having gained their sea-legs at least for the time being, life soon settled to a daily routine. They hardly noticed that they were all adjusting to walking on sloping decks which were often slippery, to ducking through low doorways, and to always holding on to the stair rails.

Jennie was now enjoying every aspect; ironically, in view of their far-off destination, she was even excited by the sight of the faint line of French coast on the distant horizon.

Later off the island of Madeira a homebound vessel drew close. The ships exchanged signals, with the intention that news of the *Lammermuir*'s steady progress would be relayed home, eventually to reach Mr Berger; the good news did arrive, and was duly reported in the third *Occasional Paper*, by which time, of course, they were much further on.

Hudson Taylor knew a good daily routine would be a multiple blessing, warding off boredom, while on the positive side lending a sense of achievement and team spirit; he and Maria got down quickly to teaching Chinese. As usual he was revitalised by the sea voyage; Maria was still far from well.

Jennie worked hard at furthering her Chinese – both in 'characters and colloquial', as she reported to her parents. Not all the party were as yet so ready to tackle the difficult study of the characters. Mr Taylor even gave Jennie and one or two of the other ladies some early lessons in Greek.

Far from the boredom of an easy passage, Jennie noted that if anything there was too much to do – and so much to disturb one's concentration: just watching the beauty of the waves was for her a major distraction. Loving every fascinating minute, she left nothing out of her observations. The weather, even the heat when it came, the bird life, the increasingly exotic fish and marine mammals which seemed to gain in size as they travelled south – all were reported on with enthusiastic detail. The moonlit nights on deck, her comfy quarters – she wrote glowing accounts of almost every aspect of the voyage, ever ready should an opportunity of a mail drop come their way. The sheer exuberance of her descriptions went way beyond any sense of obligation to reassure her parents of her well-being. 'Who would not want to be a missionary?' she exclaimed to her journal.

The journey to China would in fact never be as long again. Within three years the Suez Canal, for so long just a glint in the eye of every mercantile trader, would be the route of choice. But for now, the long journey round Africa served its purpose, with ample time for in-depth language study, team-building and Bible training.

But there was one adjustment Jennie and several others wished they could make.

For a start, most agreed they were too well fed. There was meat three times a day, and at the midday meal, often a choice. Science had moved on since the days of scurvy on the long passage, and passenger ships prided themselves on serving sumptuous meals with abundant fresh food. There was plenty of fruit, some canned or bottled – and the meat, of course, came aboard alive and in cages. Jennie imagined her parents staring at their plates at mealtimes, wishing their daughter could have similar fare – little realising she probably was!

But the main problem was that meals were just too leisurely. Captain Bell was used to having passengers with time on their hands; seated at table with them he purposely allowed two or even three hours for the expansive midday meal. His table companions were eager to get on with the next task however. The Captain just was not used to this new passenger work-ethic.

Back in her cabin, Jennie made suggestions to her journal: 'Soup and dessert we could well dispense with', she declared.

Her letters, yet to leave her cabin, included caring remembrance of those at home: she mentioned many by name, including friends at the chapel. She was concerned about Grandfather Faulding, now living alone in remote Swinefleet. She was so pleased she had made the effort to fit in a visit to Yorkshire before departure. And what about her Uncle Francis? Had he and Aunt Eliza returned yet to Australia? She expressed sadness at the thought of how different her three siblings would look when she saw them again; the one who would change most in her long absence would be little Alfie: the baby whom Mr Taylor had once rocked to sleep was now entering his teenage years.

From the start of the voyage daily prayers before breakfast had been a priority. The Saturday afternoon prayer meeting must continue also – united in heart with the one taking place in the Bergers' home at the same time of day. From its beginnings in Beaumont Street, the dedicated group had prayed for opportunities to share the gospel with the crew of any ship which would eventually take them to China; now the moment was here, and a service was started to which they could invite captain and crew. Captain Bell was already a practising Christian, so was sympathetic; he suggested members of the crew would be more likely to attend if the service were in the stern cabin, rather than in full view on the upper deck. Gradually the men came.

From first coming on board the team had consistently shown friendliness and practical assistance to the crew; now they began to notice a softening in attitudes, both generally and in response to the gospel. Some of the men were coming from a position of extreme opposition and coarse mockery; they were finding perhaps it was not so bad after all to be transporting a shipful of hymn-singing missionaries. When Mr Tosh, the second officer was converted, there was celebration indeed! As the weeks wore on there was almost a revival atmosphere, so many were the conversions among the crew, with miraculously changed lives, tempers and language, to match.

Toward the end of July, they rounded the Cape of Good Hope, at the southernmost tip of Africa. After two months at sea, and of course without any news from home, Jennie was still striking a completely positive note in her letters. She reported no disagreements among the team – but, in fact, Mr Taylor knew grievances were beginning to surface. His key to maintaining peace at this stage was diversification of roles. One or two of the ladies were in danger of being held back in their learning, for the sake of the more practically minded men. So, they were given the extra task of teaching the non-literate members of the crew to read and write. The crew was multinational, but Louise Desgraz was Swiss, and something of a linguist, and Jennie had studied German, so new skills came to the fore. The men of the team, on the other hand, had no shortage of outlet around the ship for their mechanical, carpentry and blacksmith skills. For his part Hudson Taylor was kept busy treating sicknesses and minor injuries among passengers and crew. So opportunities for being of service continued, and harmony was thus maintained among the missionary band. Jennie reported to her parents that, contrary to initial concerns, the single men had been no problem!

They had been sailing for three months – three endlessly fascinating and invigorating months according to Jennie, who claimed not even to have missed a single meal – when it was time for their planned one-day stopover. On 29 August they docked at Anjer on the island of Java, then part of the Dutch East Indies; they had barely a fifth of their journey left to complete.

For the first time Jennie saw people who didn't look like her: in her letter home she couldn't resist commenting on the strange appearance of the local 'Indian' population. She thought the waterfront Dutch architecture spoilt the overall first impression; it was doomed to disappear anyway within twenty years, swept away in the devastating tsunami which would follow the eruption of Krakatoa.

Small boats quickly came alongside them, their owners shouting their wares. Jennie didn't like the look of the caged chickens on offer, relieved they still had some left of their own. On the dockside, however, there were quantities of much more enticing exotic fruit for sale; they enjoyed particularly the novelty of drinking milk from coconuts.

But as they walked along the street, their greatest sense of anticipation also threatened to be the most enormous letdown: they each hardly dared mention to another their secret dread.

They need not have worried. As they handed over at the post office their own considerable mail, every heart rejoiced at the sight of letters from home waiting for each one. Lessons had clearly been learned since Hudson Taylor's lone departure more than a decade before.

They retraced their steps to the waterfront, trying the street food with hopeful impunity as they went. Down on the beach they sat and read their letters. The hinterland looked like dense jungle, but Jennie, recording her first sighting of an alligator, noted the peace and beauty of the beach, unspoilt by tourists such as would crowd the popular resorts at home.

In the weeks before arriving in Java, a delicate theological question had arisen among some of the team. The subject of believers' baptism was being discussed, and three of the single ladies had approached Mr Taylor on the matter. Mary Bowyer and Jane McLean, both Anglicans, and Elizabeth Rose, Mr Meadows' bride-to-be, a Methodist, had all been baptised as infants. There was no coercion, apparently, and they were clearly persuaded in their own minds that they would like to be baptised again, this time as believers. Rather than waiting until arriving among the missionary community in Shanghai, a private ceremony was planned while at Anjer. Some suitable fresh water was found – not difficult in such a steamy equatorial paradise with a downpour nearly every afternoon – in order for Mr Taylor to baptise them. Jennie, a Baptist and therefore supportive, noted to her parents that it was as well to do this now, before those she referred to as the paedo-baptists take offence in the missionary community later. But in spite of this, the unordained Hudson Taylor did come in for later criticism, for what was considered by some to be a meaningless repeat baptism.

They were now nearing their destination; just a few more days, a week or so perhaps with a good wind, and they would at last be within sight of the Chinese shore. Excitement was mounting, and on Sunday 9 September a farewell meeting was held for the crew.

But those able to read the signs soon realised that all was not well. A strange darkness was spreading across the sky; it was getting frighteningly difficult to spot the multitudes of the region's rocky islands, each named after a ship which had previously foundered there; the background creaking and groaning of the timbers, a constant accompaniment in all but the calmest weather, was growing louder.

And the sea was growing rougher – rougher than the passengers had experienced so far. It was hard to believe that, the end almost in sight, their worst experience might still be to come. But they were in the South China Sea, notorious for merciless typhoons.

Soon virtually everyone on the ship was in survival mode. For the next three or four days, while rain descended in sheets, waves as high as houses washed over the ship, and shouted orders were hardly audible, the crew's labours were unceasing. Those well enough in the *Lammermuir* party – and that was never the full complement, but always included Jennie – were themselves constantly mending or manning the pumps, securing all moveable objects, or simply occupying and calming the four children.

Eventually relative calm, both within and without the vessel, did begin to take over. By the Saturday routine had returned, and full of joy and thankfulness the passengers were able to have their normal afternoon prayer meeting. They had not noticed before how many of the stirring hymns they loved to sing used the metaphor of storms; now their voices rose in even louder praise.

The crew surveyed the damaged vessel. The typhoon had blown them off course: they would have sailed north along the Chinese coast, between it, and the island of Formosa. They were now passing to the east of Formosa instead of the west.

There followed a week of quiet weather. There was even leisure for one or two of the team to fall out with one another again. But then it was gradually realised they were heading into yet another storm – made more deadly now by the state of the weakened vessel.

Securing All Moveable Objects (1866)

This time the danger escalated more quickly. Passengers and crew alike feared for their lives, as masts were breaking off overhead, and were either washed overboard or beginning to swing dangerously. Lifebelts were always to hand, but with seas so dangerous they would hardly have been of use. Those among the crew with a new-found faith found it sorely tested, but words of encouragement were shouted one to another above the noise of the storm, and although terrifying in ferocity, this time the typhoon passed in less than three days. On top of everything else, Captain Bell had been unwell and out of action for these apocalyptic three days.

Between the two typhoons, Jennie had suffered toothache; in the most critical moments she hardly noticed it, but in the lull it came to the fore. She asked Mr Taylor if he would remove the offending tooth. 'I think sea-life is bad for the teeth', she told her journal.

This was the first time Jennie had required his professional services; with hardly a moment's illness throughout the voyage she was usually the one who nursed others. She was amazed how busy Mr Taylor had been with minor surgery throughout the voyage: there had been abscesses, tooth extractions and splinters aplenty, and numerous accidents requiring sutures.

'Were I a sailor I would try for a ship that had a doctor' – was her delightfully naïve response in her journal following her experience of extraction without anaesthetic.

Writing retrospectively to her parents concerning the typhoons, Jennie knew they would not be able to worry. Not sparing them any detail therefore, she indulged her by now considerable technical knowledge of the structures of the ship. She knew by name which masts had fractured, and which sails had ripped. The men, she said, had been constantly knee-deep in water.

And to her journal: 'God grant that having been brought to the gates of Eternity . . . our lives may be entirely devoted to him.'

7

Picking Up the Hangchow Dialect (1866–67)

On Tuesday 25 September the sun they thought perhaps they would never live to see again rose once more, and the sea was calm. The moonlit nights returned, and slowly the *Lammermuir* limped along the final coastal stretch. On the Friday a steam tug came out to meet them; a pilot came on board, as impatient to share his slant on world events with a news-starved company, as he was to steer the ship – and at last they began to turn into the broad mouth of the Yangtze. After two typhoons, Jennie told her parents she would be 'ready to sing for joy' at the sight of Shanghai.

Within the Yangtze estuary all large vessels had to stop at Wusong, the port at the mouth of the Huangpu, a tributary flowing into the estuary. From there the remaining fifteen-mile journey up the Huangpu to Shanghai required the assistance of a tug. On Sunday 30 September, four months after first setting sail, the *Lammermuir* finally dropped anchor opposite Shanghai. Their epic journey was over at last.

As soon as he could, Hudson Taylor visited the post office to send a few brief words to London. The telegraph service was still rudimentary; the cable linking Shanghai with Europe would not be complete until 1871, so any telegram before then would be transported part way on horseback. According to Mr Berger's *Occasional Paper* number 4, news of their safe arrival reached London on 25 October. Even one month after the event, it brought massive relief to the Fauldings.

Jennie's initial impressions of Shanghai were deflating: the immediate shoreline seemed to be lined with the grandest of mansions, and the business houses of the Americans, British and French. Her heart sank as she saw western couples walking arm-in-arm along the promenade, or the Bund as it was known, the men in their tailored suits, and women in fine silks, much as they would be in Regent's Park. There were even well-tended flowerbeds, not full of roses here, but planted with sweet-smelling oleander bushes. She was not too concerned, however: wherever conspicuous wealth exists, poverty lurks in the backstreets. She knew she was about to see the real China.

She didn't have to wait long, as porters and money-changers clamoured around them on the dockside, shouting their price, with the inevitable beggars not far behind. The waterway itself was clogged with sampans, many with whole families living on board.

For most of its thousands of years of history, self-sufficient China had never considered itself in need of trade with the rest of the world. Shanghai, therefore, in comparison with, say, a typical Mediterranean port, was almost brand new. It was now quickly making up for lost time, however,

Picking Up the Hangchow Dialect (1866–67) 63

successfully trading silk, cotton, hemp, and of course tea, with the outside world.

Hudson Taylor had certainly given thought to what they would do on first arrival – but no firm arrangements were in place. He knew friends were expecting him, but if all else failed he decided they could hire a series of small boats on which to live for the time being, these being anyway what were needed for the next stage of their journey inland along the canals.

The Captain had originally planned to allow them just a week or so to unload their belongings; but now circumstances were different: the ship would need weeks of repair and refit. The passengers also would need some weeks to salvage and properly dry out their belongings. Moreover, Captain Bell knew he was deeply indebted to this unusual band of passengers for the way they had set to in the typhoons with extremities of hard work, and particularly to Mr Taylor himself, whose calming influence on the crew at the most desperate moments had prevented certain mutiny. Yes, they could use the ship for storage for as long as they liked.

This would seem the answer to Hudson Taylor's prayers – but instead, a good friend in Shanghai made a generous offer: the whole party were invited to stay, and store their entire luggage, in his spacious warehouse.

They finally took their leave of the *Lammermuir* in the November. When it came to it some, among both crew and passengers, felt as if they were parting from family members, so great had become the spiritual bond. There were some disappointments, as a few crew members, pulled by the night life of the port, appeared to go back on their conversion experiences. First Officer Brunton, whose experience was perhaps the most dramatic, was determined that would not include him, and months later back in England he visited the Bergers, still testifying to his radically changed life.

The new missionary band loaded up four large house-boats with personal luggage, leaving bulkier items stored in the warehouse. They were certainly relieved to be going. The importance of wearing Chinese dress had been thoroughly discussed months before, and the men had already shaved their heads and fixed their false pigtails, but in the sophisticated atmosphere of Shanghai, and having stepped off a ship that looked fit only for salvage, they were feeling conspicuous; they were already beginning to be labelled by the Christian community as the 'pigtail mission'.

By December they had reached the city of Hangchow, their next immediate destination. By this stage the women as well as the men all had their Chinese outfits, some purchased in towns along the way. Far from easy to start with, as winter approached most agreed the thick but lightweight layers were very welcome. Most were mastering chopsticks also. The makeover was total, just as Mr Taylor had always said it must be. For Jennie, the transformation had started on 8 November, when she reported to her parents she had had 'my hair . . . done à la Chinois'.

Jennie was happy to turn her back on the house-boats, which had managed to strain even her ability to enjoy anything novel. The passing countryside was pretty, with an abundance of azalea bushes and a riot of magnolia along the way – but the view was from low down, and anyway it had been impossible to study in the boats.

At least a thousand years older than Shanghai, and at the southern end of the ancient Grand Canal, Hangchow was something of a cultural centre, and known for its stunning location. Situated on the shores of the beautiful West Lake, and surrounded by wooded hillsides, it was unsurprisingly a favoured residence of artists. With willows sweeping the water's edge, and pagodas surmounting the hills, Jennie's first impression was it all looked so . . . well, Chinese. But with temples dotted about on the hillsides, and tombstones set as if guarding the valley, there was an alien aspect to the beauty.

On arrival Taylor went with a local Chinese friend to look for a suitable property.

As with most towns throughout the region, there were parts of Hangchow which, in spite of its beauty, had suffered terribly in the Taiping Rebellion; in some areas, buildings were in ruins, and debris lay everywhere. A large mansion was soon found, however, not much more than a shell of a building, and very dirty, but their minds almost ran away with them as they considered its potential. Once a mandarin's residence, it had something of former glory about it. There were upwards of thirty rooms, most capable of partitioning, and with space for school rooms, a chapel, a print shop, even a small hospital. This would be the CIM's first forward base, and also more permanent accommodation for some who would maintain the work there, rather than be moving inland. Mr Taylor quickly secured it with an agreed rent – and work began.

The building, No. 1 New Lane, as it became known, had a central courtyard onto which doors and windows opened, so if need be there was opportunity for fresh air and exercise without going into the street. Many Chinese homes were smaller versions of this: high walls with huge gates, and no windows onto the street – rather like little prisons, Jennie observed. But she soon learned the inner courtyards were hives of activity; in fact, the whole world to some women.

The men set to and hung artificial ceilings below the rafters, and built wooden partitions wherever needed, almost doubling the number of rooms. It was decided that as well as the base for the Taylor family, and temporarily for others of the party, it would be a more permanent home for Jennie, Emily and Susan Barnes, the Irish member of the group.

Jennie, with her eye both for detail and for the positive spin, described the repair and fitting out process to her parents. Technical skills among the men and homemaking abilities among the women were reaping rapid transformations. The furniture was still basic, she said – trestles for tables and spare doors for beds, but considerably 'civilised by tablecloths, soft furnishings, and antimacassars' brought from home. Some small items of furniture were constructed from bamboo; she went on to explain the versatility of this product, from which everything from rope and paper to scaffolding poles could be made. It provided 'nice' matting for the floor and, even, the tender shoots could be eaten.

Their own private bedrooms were gradually taking shape, shelves and cupboards appearing as if from nowhere. Maps and prints, brought from home or purchased locally, took their place on the walls, and soon 'clocks were ticking everywhere'. She even had a washstand at the foot of her bed. She told her parents she felt like a queen!

But Victorian propriety prevented any description of toilet facilities. Mrs Faulding was left wondering if this was one privation too far. On the ship she well knew what had been involved, as she had actually seen them!

Picking Up the Hangchow Dialect (1866–67) 67

There was much more in the way of household goods still to be retrieved from the Shanghai storage, of course. They were particularly looking forward to reclaiming the things that had travelled, and presumably survived two typhoons, inside Mary Bausum's piano!

Later Mary, having rejoined her family in Ningpo, enjoyed playing her longsuffering piano – albeit out of tune.

Jennie knew her letters conveyed her unfailing enthusiasm; it occurred to her that her parents might think she was hiding something, so by way of balance she decided to tell them about the rats. They got everywhere, she said; after nibbling at her atlas they ate candles and clothing – but they were equally happy consuming refuse – of which there was plenty in the street.

There were other hazards on the streets of Hangchow. It might be a place of beauty, but it had its prosaic areas, with narrow sometimes smelly thoroughfares. There were drainage gulleys, in reality open sewers, often blocked with a decaying animal carcass, running down either side of the street; these had to be stepped across in order to reach a shop or house. This made a considerable obstacle course for those carrying the sedan-chairs, the favoured mode of transport in Hangchow, or the men carrying heavy pans bouncing as they swung from a yoke across their shoulders. When the Mandarin himself came through, his chair would be held aloft, with outrunners shouting to clear the way, using their pigtails as whips.

In spite of these alien sights, smells and sounds, Jennie was anxious to get out and about. She had made a start whenever the boats had been tied up, delighted beyond words when she found she could, in a rudimentary fashion, already make herself understood. But now in a more static situation they must 'lie low' for a while, giving the neighbours time to adjust. They were a large company, and for all that they were dressed in the right clothes, they were still 'foreign', and could still be perceived as a threat. There was plenty for them all to be getting on with indoors.

But when the time eventually came Jennie made friends quickly; living up to the meaning of her Chinese name – Miss Happiness – she seemed quite naturally to attract children around her. Then little by little the women became curious, and she started conversations with them also. As the women grew bolder, their endless questions became more obtrusive: they seemed particularly interested in how much everything cost! 'They look at me closely to see if I am the same [as they are]', Jennie reported. Before she knew it, she was picking up the Hangchow dialect.

The women all smoked pipes, she told her mother. On her first tentative visits to their homes, she was almost overcome with coughing. They also had little brass warming-pans which they filled with hot coals to put their feet on. Jennie thought these were a splendid idea, and planned to send one home for her mother. When Mr Taylor heard about it, however, he said there was no need to do that, as his mother had three, back home in Yorkshire, and would happily send one of hers to Mrs Faulding.

Eventually the day came when Jennie invited her new friends into the ground floor of the 'mansion'; they brought their pipes and foot-warmers with them. They even brought their own refreshments, in the form of their little individual teapots filled with milkless, sugarless tea.

Picking Up the Hangchow Dialect (1866–67)

Jennie explained to her parents the roles of their various servants: a cook, a washer, a tailor, a water carrier, also a boy! It seemed a lot, but they were not expensive, she said, and were very reliable. They also provided more opportunities both for language practice, and for sharing the gospel message; and in the early days when contact was minimal, they were a link-in with the local population.

They also formed a core congregation for the regular Chinese language prayers held in the newly constituted chapel. They were attracted at first as much as anything by the sound of singing, to the accompaniment of Mr Taylor's miracle harmonium, now the incredible veteran of three trans-world voyages and two typhoons! Jennie and Emily soon had two Sunday schools going, one for children and one for adults; they began to teach the servants to read using Hudson Taylor's Chinese New Testament, written in Romanised script.

In writing to her parents Jennie was beginning to bemoan the long delays in correspondence; she still did not know for sure how they had reacted to the news of the typhoons. But she was delighted to have started receiving outdated but regular copies of *The Illustrated London News.*

In fact, Jennie was aware she probably received more mail than others; Mrs Berger wrote faithfully to each of the ladies, but in order to boost Emily's meagre postbag, Jennie suggested to her parents they might like to write separately to Emily occasionally. She worried too about Emily's diet, asking her parents to send biscuits for her, as she didn't get on with rice. Nowhere near as robust as Jennie, she did eventually settle to the food, much to everyone else's relief.

In the February of 1867 a baby girl, Maria, became the newest member of the Taylor family. Mrs Taylor had been pregnant for almost the whole of the sea voyage. As usual, the pregnancy had not been easy, but it was a joy to see both mother and baby now doing well. Chinese babies were wrapped up rather than washed, and curious visitors thought baby Maria would catch cold, with too-frequent bathing. The new arrivals on the other hand thought it odd that Chinese babies' bottoms were always exposed! When they saw toddlers in the street similarly clad, they had to concede it was at least a creative approach to certain other problems!

It would soon be the first anniversary of leaving Britain's shore. The first *Lammermuir* betrothal took place at this time – between Miss McLean, one of those who had been baptised on Anjer, and Mr Sell, the gardener. But very sadly the marriage was not to be; John Sell became ill, quickly deteriorating, and tragically died of smallpox on 18 May.

But for Jennie personally, life was unfailingly good. By the June of that year, she had started a boys' day school. She also reported to her parents that with four local homes now open to her, 'There is nowhere I would rather be'.

In the July, their old friend Wang Lae-djun was appointed pastor of the embryonic New Lane church. This, of course, was someone the Fauldings had known well; his name would crop up frequently in her correspondence from now on. The other name they became used to in coming months was that of Ah-Lo-Sao. She was Jennie's first real Chinese friend. Unable to have children, she had been rejected by her husband, who moved on to a new relationship. Perhaps through her own needs she quickly became responsive to Jennie, in time developing the skill of inviting others along to gatherings also.

The summer heat was now building, and the Taylor family and other members of the team planned a retreat. Barely five miles away, but up in the hills, and with the song of the birds, a constant breeze, and fresh water that was mountain sweet, Pengshan was a place of recuperation and refreshment. This was the furthest Jennie had travelled since arrival. Typically, once again the journey fascinated her, as they passed first the paddy fields, with the blindfolded buffalo driving the water wheels, then on up through plum and apricot orchards, until they arrived at their destination, an old abandoned temple; here they 'camped', with their own bedding. They also brought their cow with them, and the servants, of course, who could easily return by boat for anything they might have forgotten in Hangchow. All around the old temple the breeze shook the feathery leaves of the gingko trees, and wafted the intoxicating scent of the wild rhododendrons right into the building. Jennie had seen examples of both, she commented to her parents, cultivated in parks and gardens back home – but here they were growing 'everywhere'. She was not so keen, she continued, when Mr Taylor produced the shotgun given him by Mr Berger, but his resurrected country skills did enable him to bag some tasty red pheasants.

And what a relief it was for the ladies to roam about outside without needing to be accompanied by a servant! 'Everyone is feeling revivified', Jennie finished her description with a flourish.

But then in the midst of blessing, searing tragedy struck again. Young Grace Taylor, the eldest of the now five children, suddenly began to grow listless. There was then a fever, and she complained of worsening headaches. Mr Taylor prescribed what he could for what he said was meningitis, but in spite of everything it was as if she somehow slipped through their fingers. She died on 23 August.

Anxious to avoid the gaze of superstitious Chinese, with their rumours of foreigners killing babies, they smuggled her small body back to Hangchow, hidden inside a bath. Lae-djun, himself heartbroken, lovingly prepared and lacquered a little coffin. He knew Grace so well, having looked after her on that first journey home to England, and wouldn't hear of anyone else doing it. In a tearful ceremony, the coffin was bricked up in a little house in Grace's favourite corner of the garden. In time it would be reburied in a foreigners' cemetery.

8

Loving Every Minute (1867–68)

Jennie, whose own day-to-day life was proving so rewarding, was nevertheless deeply moved as she considered the quantity of pain in the lives of some others – especially the longsuffering Taylors. Neither did Emily have an easy ride. She would feel the loss of Grace more deeply than Jennie, having shared a cabin with the little girl throughout the long sea voyage.

Emily, albeit still with health challenges, had now found her niche: she was beginning to fulfil a demanding secretarial role alongside Hudson Taylor, additionally carrying a considerable burden of administration whenever Mr Taylor was away travelling. Jennie, on the other hand, was doing precisely what her elite professional training had prepared her for – and she was loving every minute.

She wondered, however, about the way some of her fellow missionaries did not make it easy for themselves. Along with the majority of the team, she was completely settled on the general usefulness of adopting Chinese dress. The ladies, led by Maria, had thought carefully: Chinese women were often not respected by their men, and Mrs Taylor at first wondered whether they, the *Lammermuir* women, would also lose respect in the community, if they wore Chinese clothes. But finding themselves so quickly inside the women's homes, they need not have worried. Most of the men too, as they began to travel, found they were better received in Chinese garb. 'Even the dogs left off barking at us', one of the men wrote to Mr Berger.

So, there was both shock and amazement when one or two members of the company suddenly appeared one day in western dress. What were they thinking of? After all, the makeover had been going so well. The perpetrators did have a defence – that better language skills were expected of them when dressed as Chinese, so in effect they felt safer for the time being retreating into western clothes. But surely, Jennie continued the discussion with her parents, external differences should always be lessened as much as possible, so the audience can concentrate more on what is said, rather than on what is worn.

Part of the problem stemmed from unhelpful observations being made by two ordained Anglican missionaries, George and Arthur Moule, settled with their families and working in Ningpo.

The *Lammermuir* party had enjoyed good relations with them to start with; but as discontent began to smoulder among some members of the team over Chinese dress, George Moule, himself invariably immaculate with his clerical collar, picked it up. He began to provide a listening ear for complaints against Hudson Taylor's leadership. 'They don't always understand our ways, as we are not church people' was Jennie's initial generous appraisal. 'But they're not bigoted' was a conclusion she later chose to revise. George Moule soon discovered that at least two of the party were indeed church people! Why did Mary Bowyer and Jane McLean not come with letters of introduction to him as the local Church Missionary Society representative, as convention would dictate? In fact, these two had had some training with William Pennefather, the Anglican vicar with whom the team had enjoyed such warm and mutually supportive relations in London. Here, Moule contended, was where the problem lay; they should not have joined the CIM in the first place. George Moule was to suffer an even greater cataclysmic blow, however: someone leaked to him that Mr Taylor, the unordained nonconformist, had had the audacity to baptise these two young ladies on the way over. The Anjer chickens had indeed come home to roost.

But as appalling as these misdemeanours seemed to Mr Moule, as far as he was concerned, he had discovered an even worse offence on the part of the somewhat maverick Mr Taylor, and a further nail for the CIM coffin.

The criticism was based on the supposition that Hudson Taylor was far too intimate with the single ladies under his roof.

Mr Taylor had promised the Fauldings that their daughter, and for that matter Emily also, would always live as part of the family. Now ironically this was, in Mr Moule's eyes, the cause, if not of gross sin itself, then of serious ongoing temptation. And what conclusions might Chinese onlookers draw? Single women generally were anathema to the Chinese, and if living with a married couple might well be considered concubines.

To be fair to George Moule, he had been receiving a steady diet of biased information from the *Lammermuir* discontents. He also felt concerned for appearances among the local western Christian community, as well as genuinely believing he had a sense of responsibility towards Hudson Taylor – but he was also reaching the point of feeling it was time Taylor was recalled!

The criticism was directed at Hudson Taylor himself, and the impropriety of being doctor, pastor and leader to the single ladies within his household to whom he was presumably also close emotionally. But to Emily and Jennie it was like a personal affront. The thought that anything as innocent as the occasional fatherly goodnight kiss should have sounded any alarm bells was deeply shocking. Emily particularly was distraught, and her natural tendency to self-blame came to the fore. Her behaviour must be at fault, she confessed to her diary; she must rein herself in. But Mrs Taylor correctly identified that her own presence had not been factored in at all. Why did Mr Moule not trust the judgement of a mature and contented wife, who herself had had a hand in the household arrangements?

But Mr Taylor decided they must choose the lowly road: he asked the single ladies of the household each to prepare a testimonial concerning his so-called behaviour. Jennie, Emily and the two remaining Marys, Misses Bell and Bowyer, wrote out their statements on the matter (the third Mary, Mary Bausum, was now living with relatives in Ningpo). They were more than happy to testify that all behaviour within the household was beyond reproach – but it was crushing to watch their 'dear Mr Taylor' take criticism from an older, more senior member of the missionary community, one whom they had respected when they first arrived.

Loving Every Minute (1867–68)

Jennie recognised Hudson Taylor's diplomacy and leadership skills were now at full stretch. Issues such as a return to western dress betrayed not only a difference of opinion; it was actually a breach of trust, of the unwritten pact between the members of the team and their leader.

Ever the optimist, Jennie was sure things would improve when 'each had their own sphere of work, and distances between them were greater'. Conveying negatives to her parents inevitably led on to her expressing by contrast the riches in her own heart, as she would pour out on paper her love for her heavenly Father, and for China. 'If I could live fifty lives, I would live them all for poor China, in its terrible destitution.' And later: 'How can I ever thank you enough for letting me come?'

The Revd and Mrs George Moule were due home on furlough. A flurry of letters passed across the globe as the Taylors, totally discreet at first, decided it was time to inform the 'home team' of their troubles. Mr Berger understood, assuring them Mr Moule would not be able to do any further damage at home. Jennie wrote to her parents similarly, enclosing a plan of their premises to aid the defence, and was eventually reassured to hear her parents would not be listening to any of his negative rumours.

In other ways, these were times of extraordinary blessing. Under Pastor and Mrs Wang, a truly Chinese church was coming into being – in tandem with Mr Taylor's clinic. He treated a plethora of medical conditions, and performed minor surgical procedures under chloroform. Opium addicts always seemed to be falling into some category needing attention – and they were never turned away.

(Expensive imported opium was now being superseded by cheaper brands grown within China. The local squalid dens where the debt-burdened poor nightly smoked themselves into oblivion were not yet losing their trade.)

A new couple, John and Margaret McCarthy, had arrived from Britain; willingly adapting to all things Chinese, they were fitting in beautifully. Older and more mature than some of the *Lammermuir* team, they were accompanied by their four children. Mr McCarthy was soon able to run a modified dispensary when Mr Taylor was away.

On Sundays in the chapel there was often standing room only (women on one side, men on the other). Mr Taylor would start the service by standing on a chair, so as to be seen by all, and go on to explain they worshipped no idols, only the one true living God who is invisible, but present by his Spirit among them.

Yet perversely rumours were circulating; more opposition was felt from some of the local community – as if the team hadn't given themselves enough internal problems. Now the most bizarre lies were spreading: the foreigners killed babies, poisoned their patients, cut out eyes. It didn't seem to matter that not a single case could be substantiated. With experience, however, came the knowledge that these types of criticism were common throughout China among the poor, uneducated population, so susceptible to prejudicial conspiracy theories.

And, of course, Jennie's school work continued; she and Mary Bowyer, her able assistant, now had about fifteen regular attenders. She described to her parents how the little boys tended to shout out answers all together at the tops of their voices. In fact, she said, they were only really quiet when writing.

Meanwhile, Mrs Taylor had started a 'school' for women. It mainly involved needlework classes, with the women being read to while they sewed. But at the end of the day, when her little boys had finished school, Jennie would sometimes give reading lessons to the women. She was mastering the written Romanised version of the Hangchow dialect – much as had been done with the Ningpo dialect.

Towards the end of 1867 William Rudland, one of the *Lammermuir* blacksmiths, proposed to Mary Bell, the Taylors' children's nurse. So Jennie had been right: the men were quite understandably choosing their future brides from among the *Lammermuir* party. She would definitely be keeping her head down as far as that was concerned. This betrothal, however, unlike the first, ended in great joy for all, when the wedding took place on Christmas Day.

This their second Christmas was more organised than the first; Mr Taylor had bagged some pheasants, venison was purchased from the shops, and plum puddings arrived from home! Jennie had also requested small gifts for her new friends. 'Don't send soap', she advised her parents, 'this will just create a need'. Instead, she asked for one-off trinkets: a kaleidoscope, perhaps, a jar of sweets, or a small framed picture of the Queen. It must have been the nostalgia of Christmas that triggered that triplet of Victorian obsessions, namely technology, royalty and sugar! Just for the day, and as a sign of settled contentment, they relaxed back into western dress.

The *Lammermuir* men were all gradually moving inland. Hudson Taylor's original plan had been to send single women inland also; he knew they were more than capable. He had to look no further than among his own household, particularly Jennie, to see the singular success of their ministry (indeed, he was 'strongly inclined to consider it the most powerful agency at our disposal'). To his consternation, however, no young married couples wanted to share their small and somewhat intimate homes with single women. The women could not live on their own, so a clear message was conveyed to Mr Berger, much to Taylor's regret, saying no more single women were to be sent out for the time being. The Bergers' extensive country home, meanwhile, was overflowing with all the work of running the Mission. They themselves were almost stretched beyond endurance with administration, and there were now so many candidates that some had to be lodged in the village. Perhaps it was therefore with slight relief, as well as great sadness, that Mr Berger announced in the latest *Occasional Paper* that he would not be interviewing any further single female applicants.

Jennie, however, was thrilled with day-to-day life in No. 1 New Lane. Within two years two of 'her' women were baptised, including her friend Ah-Lo-Sao. 'There is a really clear line here between believer and idolater', Jennie explained to her parents. A sign of true conversion would be the decision not to make any more funeral paper money (the money that was burned when someone died, in the belief it was needed in the afterlife). As a cottage industry, it was the main means by which poor women could support themselves – so it was far from easy for Ah-Lo-Sao and others like her to give it up.

Loving Every Minute (1867–68)

Jennie's ability to befriend the women was nothing short of amazing. 'I have only to go out and pass along the street, and houses are opened to me.' She regretted only the time constraint, with her ever-present desire to divide herself into multiple people!

One day she found herself in an entirely new situation: one of the 'military mandarins', along with his wife, had attended a couple of meetings, and they invited Jennie to visit them back in their home.

Much preferring to sit down in the poorer homes, she nevertheless coped with the ceremony and stiffness of their palatial residence. She had previously noticed that the practice of foot-binding was less important among the ordinary women of Hangchow; almost bent double bearing their huge baskets of root vegetables, they needed the support of strong feet. But with high-born women such as the mandarin's wife, tiny feet were critical, both for marriage prospects, and to demonstrate their leisured lives. Private courtyards therefore came into their own, as on foot, the women were barely capable of venturing any further.

The mandarin and his wife asked searching questions about forgiveness. They expressed an interest in giving money for the blind who attended the New Lane dispensary, but Jennie was convinced they had been confused by some Roman Catholic doctrine, and wanted in effect to buy favour. She described the mandarin as an interesting, stout man, but 'all body and no soul'.

By the April of 1868 there had been changes at New Lane: No. 2 had been acquired, the ground floor being converted into a much larger chapel, with room for 200, and the old chapel used as an extended print room: multiple copies of *Daily Bread* in the Romanised Hangchow dialect were now flying off the press. Jennie was happy to continue as she was. Her own little room was if anything becoming more comfortable; she was gradually acquiring Chinese books to add to her considerable number of English ones – like all book lovers, she liked to be surrounded by good books. And she now had glass in her window – not the more common paper. But still, of course, it only looked inward, over the courtyard. How she would have loved a small window from which, as she said, she could peep out onto the outside world.

She enjoyed visiting Hangchow's luxurious shops, especially the silk shops, so beautifully colour-coordinated with their gorgeous dyes. There were china shops and idol shops, even coffin shops. Each had their gilded and colourful sign boards outside, creaking and swinging when the wind blew in from the lake. But she hardly bought any silks; instead, she was busy converting her redundant dresses into Chinese garments. 'The women love my silks', she wrote home.

Within just a hundred yards or so of New Lane she now had many friends with whom to maintain contact. Not all were as rewarding as Ah-Lo-Sao, who was expressing her new-found joyous faith in 'simple faith-filled prayers'.

Then in the July, Jennie had unexpected news from home: her brother William was seriously considering coming to China. He had been in correspondence with Mr Taylor, apparently. Jennie was cautiously delighted, but also concerned. She knew how pressurising Mr Taylor could be; his own sister Amelia had struggled with her brother's compelling reasoning, when she and husband,

Loving Every Minute (1867–68) 83

Benjamin Broomhall, knew in their hearts that China was not for them. But if indeed William was coming, he need have no concerns over his 'delicate lungs', since China was the best place for those with that problem, Jennie assured him. He was also considering he might come out with the Wesleyans: teetotalism and the Pledge were currently occupying his thoughts.

Also in the summer of 1868 there was a significant development in terms of members of the team moving inland, and this time it was the Taylors themselves who were relocating. Emily was going also, and Louise Desgraz, plus the newlywed Rudlands (Mary Rudland was still the children's nurse) and about six Chinese believers from Hangchow. There was no question but that Jennie with her established work in Hangchow would remain, with Pastor and Mrs Wang, and with Mr and Mrs McCarthy, who replaced the security of the Taylors.

The party travelled by boat, north along the Grand Canal, to the city of Yangchow. Once the city where Marco Polo was governor, now it had developed something of a reputation for unruly mobs.

The literati of Chinese society were genuinely concerned for the preservation of their ancient, dignified and cultured civilisation in the face of any barbarians from across the seas: in restive Yangchow, and in the oppressive summer heat, it did not take much for the mob to be incited by some well-placed rumours. The new arrivals did not even have time to settle when a menacing crowd surrounded their house. A riot was starting to build.

The final news, when it reached Hangchow, was almost unbelievable. For Jennie it was as painful to bear as if she'd been a helpless witness. Several of the party had been attacked physically, a fire had been started, and lives saved only by many having to jump out of a first-floor window. This included Emily, the two oldest Taylor boys, and Mrs Taylor – who was again pregnant.

Jennie could not bear to think of her own dear Emily being physically manhandled by a crazed Chinese. 'We hardly knew how much we valued your love', McCarthy later wrote to Hudson Taylor, 'till it was nearly lost to us'.

Nevertheless, when the authorities had quieted the city, and their home repaired, the party did settle there for a while. There had been broken bones and other injuries, but mercifully no loss of life, and in the November baby Charles Edward was born there, arriving safely in spite of the horrendous events during Maria's pregnancy.

Once again Jennie felt herself one step removed from the disasters of others. Once again she was the onlooker, the supporter of victims. It was barely more comfortable.

9

Mentioned in the House of Commons (1868–70)

The atmosphere at New Lane was subdued; everyone was quietly relieved that all were safe in Yangchow after the terrible riot. But the health of both Maria and Emily was still giving rise to concern.

Jennie's diary increasingly recorded the comings and goings of others: new missionaries would arrive, almost immediately moving on inland. Hangchow was now a hub – but she was settled. Whether it was out of duty and commitment, a sense of joyful fulfilment, an awareness of being in the heart of God's will, or submission to Mr Taylor – it was all one and the same. 'One day is very much like another', she wrote, implying contentment, not boredom. Her spirit of adventure, originally part of her calling, was now no longer dominant.

But by the autumn she and the McCarthys had moved into No. 2 New Lane. She had to admit that No. 1 had begun to feel 'desolate' with no Emily and no Taylors. But once again in her letters she was at pains to point out how comfortable she was ('I question if I have not too many comforts for a missionary') – giving detailed descriptions of her new quarters. Her ferns had made the transition well, and she had a chilli plant in her window – which faced outwards! She could now watch the geese fly over from the lake each evening. But the firecrackers, let off to appease evil spirits whenever there was a death or serious illness, now sounded louder.

The New Lane dispensary was permanently closed, now that Hudson Taylor was elsewhere. Jennie was quick to recognise the positives of this: 'We are widely known and . . . established; there are some advantages in not holding out any baits.'

She was growing increasingly at ease with Mr and Mrs McCarthy, and 'Lae-djun and his wife are such a comfort'; she was still enjoying the security her parents had requested, albeit in a different family setting. Additionally, another couple, the Judds, had arrived, and for the time being were designated to remain in Hangchow. Mrs Judd soon settled to learning the ropes alongside Jennie, at the same time as joining her team of invaluable classroom assistants. This was timely, as Mary Bowyer was often unwell, and away in Ningpo recuperating. Jennie couldn't help noticing that when Mary was absent she was the only remaining member of the *Lammermuir* party in Hangchow. But she was as content as ever, contemplating in a letter: 'I think perhaps I have better health than anyone else.'

By the end of 1868, Jennie had instituted a momentous conceptual change: she made the brave decision that 'her' school should no longer be the financial responsibility of the CIM, but that of hers personally. And in consultation with the McCarthys, it was decided that the work in

Hangchow should no longer represent the headquarters of the Mission; it should become the responsibility of those who worked there, not that of Mr Taylor, who Jennie felt lived constantly on the edge of nervous exhaustion. He was the most generous-spirited of men, but delegation just was not his strong point – with the exception, that is, of much of the administrative burden, which was part-shouldered by Emily, and his longsuffering wife. He was frequently ill, 'prostrated solely by anxiety and overwork' as Jennie put it. (He had finally been left with no choice but to dismiss from CIM membership the Nicols, the other original *Lammermuir* married couple, being the ones still in rebellion to his leadership. Two of the single women stepped down in sympathy. This was grievous in the extreme to the conciliatory Hudson Taylor.)

The Sunday school of Jennie's home church had recently remitted £10 for her support; she took this as a sign, a beginning, of being able to shoulder the financial responsibility herself. But unbeknown to her, more was to come. She learned of it via sad news from home.

Apparently, her Uncle Francis in Australia, her father's older brother, had recently collapsed and died, aged only 52. In spite of a life's work in pharmaceuticals, he had not been a healthy man. However, with no children of his own he had left a generous legacy to each of his nephews and nieces. For Jennie this meant a lifetime's modest allowance, with which she could 'do something'.

As regards the school, with increased space on the premises she was now accepting eleven boarders; she estimated each cost about £6 a year. The cost of educating the ten or so day boys, even with some food provided, was 'trifling'.

As she contemplated the very practical difference her allowance would make, her thoughts turned to a girls' school. Apart from being a cherished ambition, it would also, she knew, be a very practical solution to finding marriage partners for the young men in the church, the alternative being that parents betrothed their sons to child brides in pagan families. In fact, any concept of female education in China was ground-breaking. There was currently next to nothing being done for girls; no family would choose to waste money educating daughters – it was expensive enough just marrying them off. But if someone were willing to educate them, it would revolutionise their status; an educated female would have to be valued in her own right. In just this one small corner of China, Jennie's cutting-edge college training was about to have a profound effect.

At about this time she made the decision to stop using Confucian teaching material. It did involve her losing four pupils, but she had no regrets. Evidently on this subject there was some discussion to be had, and they were not the only mission to have to think it through. Using 'native' material inevitably equipped boy pupils better educationally, and certainly if they were to be entered for the revered national examinations – held each October and requiring vast chunks of rote learning. It was possible, some said preferable, to teach Chinese classics alongside Scripture, and it was important for intelligent pupils to appreciate the difference. But some parents were led to believe the two were therefore equal in value, and in the end, Jennie decided immature minds were not discerning enough to tell the difference.

With letters at roughly fortnightly intervals, Jennie continued to keep her parents well informed; she updated on spiritual challenges and encouragements, and gave detailed descriptions of everyday happenings.

She was committed, as she said, to being 'candid'. ('My friends the rats still visit me.') She tried not to miss out minor ailments, in case her parents suspected she was holding something back, but she maintained the device of telling them when it was over. She informed them when she had recovered from toothache, adding that she had not 'exposed myself and got ague [malaria] yet'. Even so, she requested quinine tablets, as they were expensive to purchase locally, and 'Mr and Mrs McCarthy are prone to ague'. Parcels packed with gifts or requested items were constantly arriving. No item from home was ever left unacknowledged. Tempting as it was to ignore the sorry state in which gifts occasionally arrived, she realised her parents needed to know. As a result, jars of jam now came doubly insulated, and underwear never arrived soaked in sardine oil a second time.

Her parents were as attentive as ever to the details in her letters, as demonstrated in their interest in minutiae. They invariably asked after Pastor Wang – an old friend, as far as they were concerned – and Ah-Lo-Sao, their daughter's closest Chinese friend, so now a new friend of theirs also. Jennie was deeply appreciative of her parents' intelligent interest: 'No-one else in the Mission has a mother like mine', she commented.

Her parents continued close companions to the Bergers, occasionally staying with them at Saint Hill. The waves of disaffection against the Taylors, emanating from Mr Moule, had now reached home. Most, including the Fauldings, stood unwaveringly supportive, but it was a pressure on Mr and Mrs Berger, especially as for a while it affected donations. At times exhausted, and no longer youthful, they nevertheless kept up all aspects of the work.

The Bergers had sold off the agricultural part of their land, not primarily for financial gain, but to give themselves more time for the work. This was part of the sacrificial way of life for the Bergers, who had enjoyed the farm management side of country living. With the sale of land some property became available, and the Fauldings bought a small house there. When Jennie heard about Horne Farm, as it was called, she told them she was pleased they now had somewhere that would make 'a nice retreat for a few days'. They were undoubtedly becoming more comfortably off, Mr Faulding's business having diversified into 'ornamental tuning forks', and employing an ever-growing workforce. They contemplated the possibility of his releasing himself from work altogether, in order for them to assist the Bergers on a more permanent basis.

But there was one aspect of the Fauldings' relationship with Saint Hill which was particularly interesting. Nellie, at 19, was still accompanying her parents; it was inevitable she would meet some of the young male candidates for China, currently filling the Bergers' home. Were Mr and Mrs Faulding again able to close their minds to future possibilities? When the quiet but hard-working Charles Fishe from Dublin was told his departure to China would be delayed, he was not unduly perturbed. He wanted to become better acquainted with Miss Ellen Faulding!

No sooner had the 'Moule' issue died down, than news of the terrible Yangchow attack reached Britain's shores. This did not escape the notice of the secular press; it was even mentioned in the House of Commons. There was confusion as to whether Hudson Taylor had appealed for reparations, or worse, gunboat protection – which he certainly had not. Misrepresentations and bitter arguments rumbled on for months. Mrs Faulding asked Dr Landels their minister to somehow intervene; he wrote to *The Times*, clarifying facts, and testifying to the peaceful relationships the CIM invariably enjoyed as they continued to open mission stations. He even cited the progress made by one 'who went out from my church' and had been almost overwhelmed with offers of hospitality and friendship.

Jennie missed Emily and the Taylors for her first Christmas without them. It was a cold winter: 'From top to toe the Chinese know how to protect themselves', she explained to her parents; they all appreciated the fur-lined boots, but 'ear-caps and nose-caps we have not yet found necessary'. But Jennie, the McCarthys and Mr and Mrs Wang were cheered as spring approached, and the Taylors plus Emily arrived for a brief Chinese New Year celebration. Jennie's school closed for two weeks for the festival, and for this Jennie was invited, in the company of her friend Ah-Lo-Sao, to take a short break with the Taylors, who were staying at Ningpo. The boys returned before she did, and it gave her a good idea of how her Chinese classroom and dormitory helpers coped without her for a short while. She had also recently acquired a full-time Chinese Christian teacher – whom she later declared to be 'proving himself just the man I wanted'.

She loved her holiday in Ningpo – a place she had heard so much about, and where she had so many friends, yet had never visited. It was reached largely by canal – the Fauldings received details of the journey: Chinese canals tended not to have locks; consequently, when land levels altered the canal stopped, and boats had to be carried across the isthmus of land to the next waterway, occasionally with female passengers still inside!

But generally, life did not get any easier for Mr Taylor in his considerable responsibility; there was still criticism from some quarters both at home, and more distressingly, on the field. Medically too he felt a unique burden, with so much sickness among missionaries, including his own family, and always babies to deliver. Jennie watched as he took so much upon himself, and she offered timely support to Maria where she could. The medical work was almost impossible without a partner, and there appeared to be none forthcoming from home. Dr Barnardo was still in touch, and evidently still torn, but Mr Berger wrote to say Barnado's interest in China was now coming a definite second to his magnificent work in the East End of London. But 'The leadings of God Chinaward have not slumbered in my breast', Barnardo had written to Hudson. That romantic turn of phrase to which the Victorians were so partial was obviously being well-honed for a lifetime's need to appeal for funds!

But just when many felt weighed down with burdens, in spite of the overall progress of the work, times of spiritual refreshing did come. The so-called Pietist movement in many churches back home was infusing congregations with a sense of spiritual renewal; it was accompanied by much writing on the subject. The *Revival* magazine reached China's shores on a regular if belated basis – and it began to have a startling and far-reaching effect. The McCarthys plus Jennie at Hangchow were among the first to catch this new flame of blessing, and as they wrote enthusiastically to Hudson Taylor about it, the news seemed to reach him just in time; always prone to self-condemnation, he had been sinking into a particularly deep pit of negative introspection when their letters arrived. As missionary teams continued to meet in their small groups, a renewed sense of the presence of God seemed to take over the gatherings: petty differences were settled with each other; a new joy lifted every soul. It was as if the Holy Spirit had opened the windows of heaven over them.

Back home, where rightly or wrongly the need for renewal was not felt to be so critical, there was more objectivity: the Bergers felt this new 'holiness' experience was too passive; the Fauldings thought it not entirely biblical. But Hudson Taylor's burdens seemed lighter – although they did not lessen. For the Taylor family one problem was looming, and growing ever larger. The children's education was beginning to suffer with the constant upheavals, which they anyway were growing to resent; and most threateningly of all, they seemed to be constantly ill.

Additionally, no one could now deny that Emily's health was deteriorating. There could be but one answer: Hudson and Maria made the heart-wrenching decision to send their four eldest children home to safety, and Emily, whose only known hope of recovery from the grip of TB would be the fresh air treatment of a long sea voyage, would accompany them. Plans were set in motion for the little party to depart early in 1870.

Emily's place as Mr Taylor's secretary would eventually be filled by the young but capable Charles Fishe, who was shortly to arrive on a return voyage of the *Lammermuir*.

For the time being, his love for Jennie's younger sister would remain undeclared.

By the end of 1869, Jennie's dream of a girls' school had become reality: it started with two pupils, a mother and daughter. As girls began to enrol, a woman was employed specifically to look after them. As with the boys, girl boarders were contracted or 'signed over' to the school for a specific period; this prevented parents lodging their offspring for a period of free food and clothing, then removing them for betrothal. Additionally, in the case of girls Jennie held the 'right of marriage', thus preventing parents selling their daughters to non-believers.

Now with responsibility for two schools, and with consequently more Chinese employees, Jennie's thoughts turned to wondering if there were likely to be anyone suitably skilled at home who would possibly be free to join her. It would be a close working relationship – and she felt she could never cope if the 'wrong' person came out.

But then she did think of someone.

Could her sister, Nellie, possibly consider coming out to help in the girls' school?

She knew what she was asking – she knew the cost to her parents, even with two sons settled in London, would be absolutely enormous. Letters flew back and forth. Amazingly, the Fauldings were prepared at least to talk about it. She understood that her parents' anxieties, even when proved needless, were nevertheless real to them. Also, by the end of 1869 Jennie had had her first attack of the ague. It had been only a slight attack, she informed her parents, retrospectively, of course, and she was taking 'plenty of quinine'.

Being ill was a new experience, and she resented being laid low, even for a few days.

Christmas was overshadowed by the knowledge of Emily's departure; her passage, with the children, was booked for March. They would travel by steamer via the brand-new Suez Canal, a journey round Africa being thought just too long for Emily. But even this plan, grievous as it was in many ways, was thwarted by tragedy.

Of the four children going home, Samuel was the least healthy. His tubercular enteritis would be helped by leaving China – but very sadly it looked as if he would not make it to departure; to the parents' great grief he grew weaker, and died in the February. Yet on top of this the bereft parents still must bid farewell to the other three, Herbert, Frederick and Maria. Charles, the toddler, would remain with his parents, themselves far from well. For such loving and attentive parents, the farewell was deeply painful, but nevertheless understood as the path of sacrifice; they bravely accepted it as such – knowledge of the damage such things can do to the children, so obvious to later generations, was hidden to Hudson and Maria at this time.

So preparations now had to be made. Clothes for the growing children were organised, and enough school material to keep them busy for the whole journey; Herbert, nearly 9, must not get behind in his Greek.

In the fullness of time, all three would eventually marry, and return as missionaries to China. The two boys, having given their parents their fair share of health concerns, turned out to be particularly robust; living to old age, and seeing the end of the Second World War, they were the great survivors of the family.

10

For Jennie it Would Be Life-Changing (1870–71)

In the February of 1870, Emily and the Taylors set off by canal for Shanghai. At the same time Jennie, accompanied by Mrs Wang, set off from Hangchow, also by boat. As planned, they intercepted the 'Taylor party' at the junction of canals in beautiful Suchow, the city of waterways; here, Jennie and Emily said their final and difficult farewells. Emily was looking desperately frail; she knew by this stage her body was battling with the disease that had affected so many of her family. But the journey back to Britain was mercifully shorter this time round: after entering the Mediterranean via Suez, Emily and the children were to disembark at Marseilles, where contacts of the Bergers would put them on the train. The Bergers themselves would meet Emily at Dover. The children's ultimate destination was Barnsley – but first a period of recuperation in summer sunshine in the grounds of Saint Hill would surely work wonders for the travel-weary little party. There would be gentle debriefing for Emily over several weeks – and the children, of course, would have acres in which to run free at last.

Jennie prepared her parents for the shock of Emily's appearance – made even worse, Jennie explained, by the fact she had lost some front teeth. But 'don't blame China for all her deterioration'. There was confusion in some minds as to whether the long sea and land voyage, and responsibility for three very active children, would have helped or hindered Emily's condition.

The Fauldings were still in Horne Farm, and were still integral to Mission work at the 'big house', so they were there to welcome Emily. They admitted to Jennie they were indeed shocked by her appearance, but soon settled to enjoying her company on walks round the estate. They were quite taken with little Maria, particularly, when the children came to tea in their cottage.

Emily had always been like a daughter to them – but she wasn't Jennie. Emily talked of the fact that it would probably not be long before the Taylors would also need to come home for a break. The Fauldings presumed that surely this time, their daughter would come too.

But nothing was said from Jennie's end concerning the five-year promise. She chatted on in her letters, continuing to disclose her deep contentment. The church was still growing, and in May there would be eight baptismal candidates: three of them were boys from her school.

She now had sixteen boy boarders in all, and two day boys: the girls' school was making encouraging progress also. At that time no one had any scruples about saying bright children were preferable when it came to education – after all, as Jennie discussed, you could do so much more with them!

Then in her July correspondence she shared the happy news that Mrs Taylor had been 'safely confined again'; but strangely she didn't seem to know any other details, even whether it was a boy or a girl.

Maria had, in fact, just given birth to a little boy, Noel. Life was a struggle for Noel, however, and to the distress of his already grieving parents, he only kept it up for thirteen days.

But at first Jennie knew nothing of this. The Taylors were currently based at Chinkiang, many miles up the Yangtze; at times she felt the distance from them, and the consequent delay in communication, very acutely. Although busy herself, she longed to be of more support to them, especially now they had lost the 'indispensible' Emily. Knowledge of Mrs Taylor's constant struggle with illness added to her frustration.

Then in the August, Jennie received the most terrible news of all: she could hardly believe it, after such a year of tragedy: Mrs Taylor, weakened from a major haemorrhage after giving birth, had finally succumbed to TB, the 'consumption' that had in all probability been developing for years. Aged only 33, she had died on 23 July 1870, the day after her little son's funeral – for which, although unable to attend, she had chosen the hymns.

Jennie suspected grief over the baby's death had hastened Maria's demise. Since she had first known her, Mrs Taylor had lost two babies and two children – and Jennie had no knowledge of the first loss through miscarriage. Through her tears she noted that dear Mr Taylor, although beyond himself with grief, was somehow rejoicing in Maria's present 'bliss'. But more generally there was growing concern throughout the Mission for his own physical health, now more precarious than ever. He succumbed the day after his wife's funeral to high fever, and yet another severe attack of dysentery. And he now had a motherless child to care for.

As for Jennie, she had a double bereavement: one of her little girl pupils suddenly became sick and died.

To Jennie it was as if the pupils were her own children. Already in acute grief over Maria, she nursed the child day and night, holding her tightly as she shook with fever, and giving her drinks when she could. The emotional energy she poured into caring for this little one came from deep within the chasm of loss she felt over Maria. She also shared the details of this more immediate loss with her parents. It was a relief she had something to write about. She knew next to nothing concerning Maria's passing; the frustration of this added to the pain of her sorrow.

Back in Saint Hill, the shocking news caused a blanket of near silence to descend. Emily felt the loss more deeply than anyone. On top of her own grief, she had to navigate the three Taylor children through their father's devastating letters. William and Mary Berger, now in their late fifties, continued throughout this time with the energy of a young couple; they were handling the increased workload of having to write personally to so many, following these recent events, on top of the almost impossible daily challenges of managing finances, applications, training, reports . . . but they did start to talk of encouraging Hudson Taylor to come home for a while.

But for the Fauldings, of course, there was an additional factor: so many of the team, including children, were dying. Death seemed appallingly commonplace. How safe was their daughter?

In the October of 1870 they committed their thoughts to paper: 'All our friends are anxious about you', the letter to Jennie stated. Referencing the supposed anxieties of their friends was a good way to broach the subject. As if the CIM team news was not bad enough, they had heard about the current anti-foreign troubles in China, and the massacre which had taken place in Tientsin. They had no perspective on the distances involved, and how far north the troubles were from Hangchow, nor the fact the attacks were primarily aimed at Roman Catholic missionaries, and chiefly French ones at that. Additionally at this time Louis Napoleon (III) and Otto von Bismarck were, in their different ways, each managing to terrorise Europe. Britain too began to feel threatened. The Fauldings could cope no longer; they 'begged' Jennie to come home.

At about the same time as she received their letter, Hudson Taylor, still itinerating, called in at Hangchow. This was the first time Jennie had seen him since his wife's death. Seeing him infrequently it was not easy to recognise any improvement, but he assured her he was beginning to feel stronger at last. Emotionally he was struggling, however, and had clearly slipped back from any sense of euphoria at the comforting thought of increasing numbers of his family rejoicing in heaven.

Then in the April of 1871, the Fauldings received a surprise – a personal letter from Hudson Taylor! After the transitory horror of what it might contain, they started to absorb his warm and personable words. His health was now extremely fragile, he explained. He thought he may, in the light of many issues, be coming home for a while, possibly in the July. He was mindful of the promise he had made that Jennie would be returned to them after five years; he was also mindful of his fatherly responsibility to Jennie (and Emily); but now there would be no Emily, and no member of the Taylor family, left in China.

He knew they were thinking originally Jennie would return with himself and Maria – but now in view of his 'altered circumstances' he wondered if they would consider it unseemly. However, he did admit he would appreciate her companionship on a long voyage – and, of course, she would be a help with Charles. He suggested they leave the final decision to Jennie herself, 'as she deals with God' – they should perhaps refrain from 'requiring' her to come home.

The correspondence between Jennie and her parents, however, had already taken a dip from its normal cordiality. Since the note of anxiety had entered her parents' letters, her terse replies were full of scriptural exhortations. '[God] will bring me home to you at the right time' was very difficult to argue with. How her mother's heart must have sunk when she read of Jennie's determination to stay and fulfil God's will, for the time being at least. The people are open, she said, she was still well, and she must continue the schools. 'You wouldn't want me to do the wrong thing' brought more pressure; Jennie was departing from her usual level of daughterly insight and compassion.

In January 1871, the Fauldings searched in vain in Jennie's letters for any acknowledgement that the five-year point would soon be reached. Instead, there was more upbeat news of the expanding schools. She shared that she was coming to the realisation she was more comfortable with girls – it was easier for her to pet them and play with them. Nevertheless, she gave equal teaching and administration time to both, as well as overseeing her teaching and non-teaching staff. She was now adept at arranging apprenticeships for her boys as they left. She had good business links, particularly in silk-spinning and printing, and a sound knowledge of the 'way things worked'. But there was a perceived drawback to her management of the girls' school – she would not bind feet. This practice of binding a child's toes permanently back under the foot, once begun at about 5 years, had to be continued with increased force throughout the growth period. Jennie would never submit any little girl to the accompanying pain and ulceration, let alone the lifetime of hobbling. 'My having them [both boys and girls] washed once a week too is another serious objection.' It was still believed that in winter such washing could make the children ill.

Church life, both in Hangchow and beyond, was showing encouraging signs of growth; many among both church attenders and school pupils were in Jennie's words 'awakened' to spiritual needs around them.

But church growth just seemed to increase Hudson Taylor's workload – and he was now ill far more than he was well. A return home for a while now looked very likely, and the faithful and efficient Charles Fishe was preparing to take over administrative responsibility. As if current demands were not enough, a local newsletter, the *Monthly Gleaner*, was launched, for the widespread stations to keep in touch with each other's news. (This internal publication proved to be so worthwhile that with various changes of name and format it would be continued well beyond the next 100 years.)

Mr and Mrs Meadows (Elizabeth Rose of the *Lammermuir* party) were also preparing to go home for some leave; they had experienced more than their fair share of suffering and persecution since each had set foot in China. As their departure was looking as if it would coincide with that of Mr Taylor, they made plans to sail together. It was going to have to wait until the summer, however: Hudson Taylor had midwifery commitments until then.

At around this time the Fauldings' hoped-for permanent home near Saint Hill suddenly fell through. Life was becoming increasingly difficult for William and Hannah.

It had occurred to Hudson that if Jennie did decide to go home, the presence of the Meadows on the same passage would make their travelling together more seemly. His mother had observed how his single position now rendered him both unable to care for the single women as he could with a wife by his side, and also vulnerable to gossip. Emily would be the ideal bridal solution, she suggested. But in her weakened state she could barely cope with the lively children now; fond as he was of her, Hudson knew it was unlikely she would gain stamina for marriage in the future.

Meanwhile, malaria was plaguing Jennie again; she was not currently as strong as she liked to think she was. Perhaps circumstances were coming together to indicate a change in direction after all.

The McCarthys, themselves only too aware of how debilitating the 'ague' could be, started a discussion with her about taking over her responsibilities. Teachers and other workers were in place anyway, and Mr McCarthy assured her he could handle the administration and overall responsibility for the schools.

Then out of the blue a letter arrived from, of all people, Charles Fishe, Hudson Taylor's valuable right-hand man.

The contents contained a shock, but with more than a tinge of joyous news. He wanted her to know that he had proposed to her younger sister! The Fauldings had given their consent, and Charles and 20-year-old Nellie were betrothed. This would have quite an effect on her parents; for the first time in five years, she found her thoughts were turning to home.

With just one more obstetric case awaiting him, Hudson Taylor began to pack his bags. Jennie too began to prise herself away. Ever one to consider others, she now began to pray that the homeward voyage would be so restorative that her health would not give her parents a single ground for concern.

So, the little party began to assemble at Shanghai. Hudson had to collect his young son Charles from where he was being looked after in Ningpo: father and son had not seen each other for nine months. He was also taking a Chinese worker, Li Lanfeng, on the voyage. He was the Mission's printer, but could be spared to accompany and assist Mr Taylor; there was every reason to think he would prove as vital as Wang Lae-djun had been, a decade previously.

The Meadows family – two exhausted parents with two lively children – were more than ready to leave China's shores for a while.

Mr and Mrs McCarthy accompanied Jennie to Shanghai, and Charles Fishe was there to say farewell to Hudson Taylor. There were others assembled to see them off, but Charles Fishe and John McCarthy would perhaps be shouldering the greatest increase in workload as a result of these departures; according to the words of the ever up-to-date

Mr Berger, in the March 1871 edition of the *Occasional Papers*, Charles was now officially 'Secretary to the Mission in China'.

Hudson Taylor had booked the cheapest passages he could find, which were on a 'French mail' steamer, the *MM [Messageries Maritimes] Volga*; they were due to depart on 5 August. They would be changing to the *MM Ava* at Canton, just upriver from Hong Kong, and this would then take them, via Saigon, Ceylon, Aden and the Suez Canal, finally to Marseilles. The cost-cutting Mr Taylor had booked third class – but someone felt sorry for them, and they were relieved to receive an upgrade to second.

The voyage was barely six weeks – but for Jennie it would be life-changing. She knew in her heart she would return one day to her beloved China – but what else? Since 1866 she had embraced and exulted in every opportunity and responsibility which had so far come her way, but she had nevertheless been young and carefree. She stepped aboard the *MM Volga* with a simple trust in God for what she had left behind, concerned only for her longsuffering parents waiting patiently for her at home. By the time she disembarked, she would not only be betrothed, she would be facing a future wedded to the China Inland Mission. From now on she would share concerns of finance, publicity, management, reputation, personnel . . . and a sense of responsibility for the lives of fellow missionaries in isolated and dangerous situations across a wide area of China.

She was almost 28; Hudson Taylor was 39.

11

Hudson Broached the Subject (1871–72)

On board routine was quickly established: as best they could, the little company met for prayers together every day. Of the five adults, only Li Lanfeng was really well, and someone always had to be in charge of the three children.

Being temporarily out of contact with both the UK and the China ends of the work, even the normally frenetic Hudson Taylor found himself with time on his hands. As ever, the sea invigorated him. And Jennie, as ever, enjoyed every aspect of the ocean voyage.

But the grief was still there – for all of them to varying extents, but chiefly for Hudson. Jennie longed to comfort him, but she realised something else was going on: there was an awkwardness between them not experienced before. In the confines of the ship, they were frequently in each other's company, yet not really communicating. What was happening? Hudson admitted later that his thoughts had been in turmoil.

Hudson Broached the Subject (1871–72)

Eventually, somewhere between Hong Kong and Saigon, Hudson tentatively broached the subject. His relief, on finding his developing feelings for Jennie were reciprocated, was sweet indeed. They were falling in love! A declaration of feelings cannot hang long in the air, however, without being followed by a declaration of true intent. It was still early days for Hudson: he wondered what kind of a foundation to a marriage it would be, to be 'constantly pining for a heavenly reunion with Maria'.

Maria became the centre of their conversations. Jennie too had a permanent place for Maria in her heart; she knew she could never replace her. After clearing the air concerning Maria, acknowledging they would always be able to talk about her, there seemed to them both to be no reason why they should not 'go public', and make their commitment official.

Hudson wrote to the Fauldings. The arrival of a letter postmarked Saigon or Aden would not in itself raise any suspicions to the waiting parents – but the contents shocked them both.

Meanwhile, for the rest of the journey home, prayer and conversation flowed easily between Hudson and Jennie again. Taking their turn at keeping an eye on young Charles and the Meadows children, they spent hours 'catching up'. Family intimacies would never have been appropriate before; now they enjoyed the warm trivia of getting to know each other in a different way.

As she listened to the gentle Yorkshire accent, Jennie was transported in her mind to the little shop in Barnsley: it had been young Hudson Taylor's world. There was the pharmacy counter, and the busy scene in the back parlour, visitors round the meal table, and maps of China on the wall. She was astounded to learn his parents had actually dedicated him to China before he was even born! Hudson Taylor had for a short while rebelled against his Christian upbringing, and when he eventually surrendered his life to God, it was with the radical promise to do anything, go anywhere, for him. Quick as a flash had come that sense that God spoke to him: 'Then go to China for me', he had felt God say.

Here were the makings of this single-minded man she knew so well.

He had always known he needed a life partner. It was always a respectful need, based on a desire for mutuality and unity of purpose. But from the age of 18 to just after his first arrival in China, it was a need which twice drove him beyond his normal prayerful God-dependence and caution. Almost helpless in love, not once but twice did he give his heart away, only to have to later break off a formal engagement in each case. Older friends of Amelia, both teachers from her school in Hull, first Marianne then Elizabeth had appealed to Hudson as good Christian women from respectable families. But the issue in both cases was China. Maria and now Jennie were different, wholeheartedly committed to the work in that land.

Hudson and Jennie discussed their shared Yorkshire roots in great detail, and they laughed over bizarre coincidences. Jennie's mother had been born a Taylor, of course – albeit from a different end of the country. More intriguing was the possibility that Grandma Faulding, born a Hardey in Hull in the 1790s, could have been related to the Hardys of Hull, into which family Hudson's Aunt Hannah had married. Variant spellings in surnames were not so important at that time. Could Jennie and Hudson even be distantly related? Then there was Amelia's boarding school run by Mary, another of Hudson's aunts; it was actually in Barton-on-Humber, a small community across the Humber from Hull, and a mere ten miles or so along the sparsely populated south bank of the estuary from Swinefleet, the Faulding abode.

Jennie thought fondly of Grandfather Faulding who had died in 1868, while she was away. Could the family doctor of Swinefleet even have known of the pharmacist in Barnsley? One thing was sure: Grandfather Faulding's forebears had crossed the marshes to Barnsley to hear Wesley – who was staying in Hudson's great-grandfather's cottage at the time.

There was an unspoken awareness that they were of similar social class. Both had received a thorough education at home, in both cases adequate enough for them to move on to further education. And as it happened, both had younger sisters who were sent away for school. But Jennie's parents were city-dwellers, aspirational and mobile in comparison with Hudson's family, who had stayed put in their busy market-cum-mining town for generations.

There was another letter Hudson needed to write, before they reached home. He started his letter to Emily describing the restorative aspects of the journey – but the real matter was far more sensitive: he knew Emily, particularly in her debilitated state, would find his news difficult. Her daughterly respect for Hudson Taylor could just as easily have blossomed into romantic commitment – yet on receiving the news she took her sadness to God in prayer. She had cherished a secret wish that perhaps she could have been the next Mrs Taylor, but she knew her health and strength were failing. Even so, she generously ensured her good wishes would be among the first to reach the weary but radiant returnees.

The company disembarked at Marseilles on 21 September, and four days later via Paris and Southampton they arrived in London. The new 'couple' went their separate ways, Jennie to her family and Hudson Taylor, with Charles and Li Lanfeng, to his – which ironically as well as his three older children, included Emily!

Since she had been home, Emily had taken the three children to Barnsley, leaving them there for a while with their grandparents. Now they were together again in London, awaiting the children's father. They were temporarily living in Denbigh Road in Bayswater, just round the corner from Hudson's sister and brother-in-law Amelia and Benjamin Broomhall, where Hudson and Maria had stayed when they first returned home. (Hudson's other sister, Louisa, was also married now, and living nearby. She and her husband, William Walker, had two little daughters, Alice and Winifred. The Broomhalls now had seven children, with three more still to come.)

For William and Hannah Faulding, the pent-up anticipation of seeing their daughter again had reached its climax. Jennie too, in the final few days of the journey, was beside herself with excitement at the thought of the coming reunion. There were tears and embraces at the railway station, followed by the joy of catching up with news of the rest of the family. But sadly, there were concerns also, and it wasn't long before differences began to be aired. Since hearing news of the betrothal Mrs Faulding, particularly, had struggled:

once again it seemed as if God might be asking of them just too much. Had they not sacrificed enough already? Why was it the runaway daughter of popular folklore not only joined the circus, she inevitably married the ringmaster?

But they were also fond of Hudson Taylor; they might not always back him in minor theological points, but they knew him to have been a loving husband and father. They began to warm to the idea of this future son-in-law – but they could not countenance it until a year had passed. In the coming days there were more tears, this time of frustration, as arguments went back and forth. Although technically Jennie was well old enough to marry whom she wished, and in her own timing, she was horrified to find this was causing a rift, and so soon after returning home.

The Fauldings' main point was that neither Jennie nor Hudson were currently well, and a year would give them recuperation time. This seemed eminently sensible, and surely a wait of at least a few months could do no harm?

But Hudson Taylor's argument, put in a letter to them, was also plausible: if a marriage brings blessing, as this one surely will, then is it not better to marry, and recuperate together, rather than apart? Hudson was picking up on problems in the Mission again, this time on the home front. For one, the Bergers were wishing to withdraw from the work. Backwards and forwards to Saint Hill, Hudson was developing headaches and stress symptoms. Surely the Fauldings must realise that everything about being married to Jennie would lift much of the strain. This was true, from his perspective – but theirs was of their daughter taking on greater family responsibilities for the first time – to say nothing of the level of fitness required should pregnancy occur.

Meanwhile, he altered his domestic arrangements, moving his household from the rather too expensive Bayswater home to 64 Mildmay Road, Stoke Newington. Basic domestic help was included in the rent, plus his mother came down from Barnsley to join them for a while and help with the children. This new address was conveniently near their Tottenham associates, and also their good friends the Pennefathers, William Pennefather being vicar of Islington. His 3,000-seater Mildmay Conference Hall, scene of so much blessing, was just round the corner in Newington Green. This area of North London, on the edge of town but with railway connections to various parts of the metropolis, was the neighbourhood in which they would be based, at various addresses (and when not in China), for the rest of their lives.

From here, at the beginning of November, Hudson Taylor wrote a frankly pleading letter to Jennie's parents. In the end the wedding day was fixed, to everyone's amazement, for the 28th of that month. Clearly, he had not given any quarter, and the Fauldings had graciously climbed right down. They went on to help with arrangements, bearing the cost of the entire event. Much later, Hudson Taylor had written regarding his own challenges with impatient young men: 'In matters of the heart few accept advice'!

Hudson and Jennie were married on Tuesday 28 November 1871, at Regent's Park Baptist Chapel, the Fauldings church, by Dr William Landels, the minister.

The chapel building itself had had a rather unusual history. Part of the beautiful cream-coloured John Nash Regency Terrace overlooking the eastern edge of Regent's Park, it was opened to the public in 1823 as a 'Diorama', the latest in Victorian entertainment involving illusion, as invented by Louis Daguerre. As with all Victorian novelty entertainments, it was instantly and wildly popular – but closed in 1851 when Daguerre's interest had moved on to what became known as his daguerreotype, the forerunner of the photograph, and the public conveniently transferred their interest to the Great Exhibition. The building, complete with moveable stage to aid the illusion, was subsequently bought and refurbished by a prominent Christian philanthropist, to become the 1,600-seater Regent's Park Chapel. In keeping with many other city churches of its day, it was of vast proportions (all well hidden behind the Nash façade), with tiered seating, and space for a Sunday school of 900, plus a day school, underneath. Hudson Taylor was familiar with the ornate stone pulpit; not for a moment had he ever imagined he would one day be standing in the elaborately decorated entrance hall, complete with grand staircases to left and right sweeping up to the gallery, to await his new bride.

The pressure of timing meant they were married by licence – but there was no lack of joy or celebration, and some relief for many, as the day unfolded. Not altogether surprisingly, there was no time for a honeymoon either; they moved immediately into Mildmay Road as husband and wife – plus four children. Emily was discreetly invited away on an extended holiday, and Mrs Taylor returned to Barnsley. Hudson's romantic temperament would ensure no lack of attentiveness towards his new bride; but they were together in the work now, and Jennie was every bit as keen as her husband to settle to the daily challenges. The challenges came straight away.

The Foreign Office was communicating with Mr Berger concerning the dangers of continuing the work in Yangchow – the city where the riot had so nearly cost missionary lives, and still perceived to be Hudson's permanent home in China. This was considered to be a misunderstanding, however. Hudson maintained the city was now a safe place to be: there had been no riot for some time, and they had both consular and Mandarin support to remain. This and other concerns from halfway round the globe were now part of Jennie's everyday awareness. Life was different for her in every way, but to it all she brought the same energy and enthusiasm she had shown in Hangchow.

The year 1871 had been significant in other ways. Communication with China was at long last simplified by the completion of the cross-continental telegraph cable – but as so often happens, an ease in a method of communication just leads to increased workload: issues that once had time to resolve before the Home Department even knew of them, now appeared on the horizon almost immediately. And Jennie was now joined heart and soul with the man whose responsibility it was to deal with those issues.

The newlyweds were deeply happy with each other, however, blessed by the rest they each found within their relationship, and unperturbed when the conversation occasionally turned to mention of Maria.

There was also a significant if local house move for the family; on 15 January 1872 they moved into 6 Pyrland Road, a more spacious property, and even nearer to the duck pond and village atmosphere of Newington Green. Emily moved back in at this point.

Early in 1872 also, William Pennefather invited the hitherto unknown D.L. Moody to preach at his Mildmay Conference, now held in the new Mildmay Mission Hall on Newington Green. The prominent American evangelist soon filled the 3,000 seats, as night after night he brought the challenge of the gospel to London's East End. Hudson Taylor, friend of the Pennefathers and living on the doorstep, was invited to share the platform. Moody, usually accompanied by his gifted musical friend Mr Sankey, was responsible for bringing much blessing into churches and individual lives at this time; the new 'Moody and Sankey' hymns of worship and dedication were soon being sung round home pianos and hummed at factory work benches as much as they swept through church congregations on a wave of popularity.

The long-established but recently lapsed Saturday prayer meetings were restarted in the new Taylor home. Attendance was strong as they were now living in the heart of their support base, not least among their influential upper-class friends of Tottenham and Hackney. It was from Pyrland Road that Hudson Taylor wrote his first letter in the *Occasional Paper* (number 28) since coming home. The Pyrland Road address went on CIM headed notepaper: it was now the established home HQ.

As well as being alongside Hudson in pastoral and oversight responsibilities, Jennie now had a large household to run. She wrote to her mother that 'servants are very difficult to get'. Her mother was only too aware of this, of course – and Jennie had been spoilt for domestic help in China. 'Spare' rooms in the house soon became occupied, albeit by those who were joining the work, and contributing various skills. Henrietta and Lucy Soltau, sisters first impressed by Hudson Taylor's preaching tours in the West Country, came to stay at this time, initially to attend the Mildmay Conference; but the relationship with the Soltau family proved to be strong and enduring.

Some helped on a non-residential basis, giving up time from their secular employment. One administrative helper recorded later that he was amazed at the personal interest of Mr Taylor. Although always under pressure he would often 'break off and come and find me', asking questions about publishing perhaps, or book-binding – a true polymath, Hudson had a fascination for a whole range of subjects he didn't need. Mrs Taylor often tried to curtail such late-night encounters apparently, as her husband would get so tired – but he loved to talk on.

Jennie confided in her mother about the perennial problem of persuading her husband not to take on too much. For his part, he was enjoying the security and orderliness of his new home base; it was a platform from which he launched out possibly even more often to accept invitations to speak, enjoying Lanfeng's company wherever he went. Even if there was at times a dearth of positive news from China, Hudson Taylor now had a vast store of first-hand experience with which to challenge hearts and minds. Financial giving and prayer support increased as he preached, and individuals came forward in personal dedication.

Hudson Taylor had mentioned in his *Occasional Paper* letter that the Bergers' health and strength was not what it was. The Taylors had hoped at first that the Bergers' respite visits to the seaside would mend them enough to continue, albeit in reduced capacity, but in the following *Occasional Paper* and dated March 1872, Mr Berger wrote his official resignation letter. Referring to his 'unbroken and harmonious' relationship with Hudson Taylor, he went on to report that Hudson would for the time being be taking over his role. This, of course, even if unrecognised by the Taylors, would be an incredible initial burden. On the other hand, it did suit Hudson's capacity for work under pressure, and his desire to stay intimately in touch with all that went on. Mr Berger was also at pains to point out there would be no conflict of interests, as the Taylors always received their financial support separately from the main funds.

It was a lifelong dichotomy for Hudson Taylor: should he stay at home, continuing to preach, raising both awareness and funds for the Mission? Or should he follow his heart, and return to China? Mixed in with the encouragements, there was always much cause for concern in the news which came down the telegraph wires. Charles Fishe had been seriously unwell, and funds were currently not being distributed. At a time when he was taking back the reins of the Home Department, Hudson felt out of control with the China field. There was news of sporadic persecution – but Hudson would downplay this publicly, for fear of inflaming British/China relations. Jennie was only too aware of the delicate tightrope her husband walked. They felt too the pressure of family matters: Charles was disappointed to hear that the Fauldings were still reluctant to release Nellie to come out to be by his side.

In a further communication, in the same *Occasional Paper* which carried Mr Berger's resignation, Hudson Taylor confided that for the foreseeable future he thought he and his wife might be dividing their time between England and China, possibly in a fifteen-month rotation.

But to leave England's shores at all at the moment was looking impossible. Who could he possibly leave in charge?

Throughout the summer months of 1872 an answer did at last start to take shape.

12

Her Calling Was Now Very Different (1872–74)

It started with an approach from a Richard Hill, civil engineer, architect and long-term supporter, who happened to be married to a third Soltau sister. He was joined by Henry Soltau, brother to the sisters, and together they offered to function as honorary secretaries (Hudson Taylor remaining officially as director) as part of a Council of Management. As such they were joined by five others, one of whom with a background in business management made an ideal treasurer, and another, George, yet another Soltau sibling, was appointed as candidate secretary; they were all strongly committed Christian men with a deep respect for Hudson. (As trustees they would also be responsible for money left in Maria's will for the children's education, and for the investment of Jennie's inheritance from her uncle.) Emily was still carrying much secretarial responsibility, in spite of declining health. Additionally, Henrietta Soltau looked as if she were becoming an indispensable fixture in Pyrland Road. Emily and the 'well-educated' Henrietta got on particularly well.

The sheer size of the team, and the breadth of skill and experience, all demonstrated volubly the burden William and Mary Berger had been carrying. Jennie, particularly, was full of thankfulness for this radical change of management style, which would take so much off her husband's shoulders.

Additionally, and wisely, a Council of Reference was set up, boasting redoubtable establishment names such as Barnardo, Guinness, Landels, Pennefather, Lord Radstock and the Marquis of Cholmondeley.

As the strong if inevitably male team came together, and the Taylors' health and strength returned, so the way seemed open for a return to China. It was time to obey the call of their hearts once again.

In August of that year (1872) they shared with both sets of parents the plan for a possible October return. The way was now clear, they explained, as a good professional team was coming together to look after the home base. It was at least some consolation to the Fauldings to realise that, in this or in any future return to China, Jennie would surely never again have to set off without a husband by her side.

Hudson Taylor commenced a final round of visits and preaching engagements – in places as far away as Dundee, Liverpool and Kendal.

Meanwhile, Jennie was giving increasing attention to what was happening back in Hangchow, according to latest news in the *Occasional Paper*. Growth in the work was a particular encouragement, with the McCarthys and Pastor Wang Lae-djun having opened more stations around the area. She began to feel excited. Refreshed in body and spirit, she was now looking forward to their return.

But then, strangely, just as her excitement began to mount alongside preparations, a new weariness started to develop. It didn't take her long to realise – in spite of her age, as she thought – that there must be another little Taylor on the way. She was thankful God was bringing this extra joy into their lives, but the weariness took the edge off her excitement. 'It seems as if we ought to go', she wrote somewhat flatly to her parents.

Li Lanfeng returned to China in the September, and departure date for the Taylors was 9 October. Hudson's sister Amelia and husband, Benjamin Broomhall, with their large and growing family, had now moved to a spacious house in Godalming, Surrey. The four Taylor children were sent to stay with the Broomhalls in Godalming, in order to ease the parting when it came. Hudson found this very painful.

They were to be 'seen off' from Charing Cross Station. When it came to the actual day, the station was particularly busy: it was all they could do to keep control of their many items of luggage. With the chaos at the ticket barrier Mrs Faulding lost her handbag, and Mr Taylor senior, always one to hang back anyway on these emotional occasions, never got through to actually see his son off.

Richard Hill had gifted them the untold luxury of second-class tickets all the way through to Marseilles. Additionally, they had discovered the *Messageries Maritimes* French line offered for minimal extra cost to carry passenger luggage from Dover all the way to Marseilles, while passengers travelled overland through France. This was definitely worthwhile: Hudson considered coping with quantities of luggage on the overland trip nothing short of 'embarrassing'.

In Marseilles they boarded the *MM Tigre* where they settled into their prosaic third-class accommodation: Hudson and Jennie had to separate into dormitory-style compartments. They again travelled via Port Said and the Suez Canal, Aden and Singapore. Hudson commented that they had left Europe, called in at Africa, and were now in Asia, all within a span of three weeks. 'Is not travelling now easy?' he declared.

With leisure to write to parents when once on the boat, they discussed in contemplative mood how wonderful it would be when goodbyes no longer had to be said. As well as now older parents, they were thinking also of Emily. Would they ever see her again? With frequent stops they could post more letters. They constantly asked about family at home, Jennie being particularly mindful of the wrench for her parents once again. Her sister was still waiting to marry Charles Fishe; both Hudson's sisters were pregnant.

And Jennie too, in true Taylor fashion, was pregnant for the voyage – which of course was another concern for her longsuffering parents. She was more inclined to travel sickness as a result, but she and Hudson agreed, considering her condition, she was able to enjoy the voyage. For his part Hudson, normally revitalised by a sea trip, was missing the experience of a clipper in full sail. He was almost twenty years older than when he first set out for China.

But excitement grew as they neared their final destination. They stopped off in Hong Kong to see the grave of their brave, enterprising but sometimes naïve predecessor, missionary pioneer Karl Gützlaff. As Hudson Taylor was just beginning to dread the organisational workload awaiting him – he drew inspiration from Gützlaff's vision.

Almost the whole of the November edition of the *Occasional Paper*, number 31, consisted of Hudson Taylor's lengthy exhortational and pastoral letter, written from the ship. He warmly commended his new Council of Management to his readers. The short introductory letter, normally written by William Berger, was this time from Richard Hill and Henry Soltau. They wrote it as from Pyrland Road, now referred to as the office of the Mission – it was, of course, still the Taylors' only home, as well as being Emily's, Henrietta's and the Taylor children's abode. The longstanding Saturday afternoon prayer meetings would also continue at this address.

On the Taylors' first wedding anniversary they dropped anchor in Shanghai harbour, and Charles Fishe was there to meet them. Rather typically for Hudson Taylor, they were not really sure where they would be heading first – in all probability Ningpo or Hangchow. Jennie couldn't wait to see her beloved Hangchow again.

Charles, whom everyone now called Charlie, had been getting on famously in Shanghai; now fully recovered from his illness he was busy and fulfilled, faithfully continuing the administration of the Mission, and keeping up with writing the *Monthly Gleaner*. His plan was now to remain in China – but what about his darling Nellie? Mr and Mrs Faulding were still cautious; Jennie reverted to her somewhat terse tones reminiscent of when her parents were begging her to return from China: 'God will help you to give her up', she wrote home.

But there was one shock which greeted the Taylors: Charlie was back in western dress. Whilst this was understandable in cosmopolitan Shanghai, they were initially disappointed to realise it was no different when he travelled inland. But ironically, the Taylors found themselves immersed so quickly in the challenges awaiting them that they had no time to be fitted out before their onward journey: they too were still in western dress when they reached Hangchow. Jennie, buoyant as ever, was amused by the novel experience this afforded, as the ladies gathered round to peer under her skirts and examine her petticoats.

She was both relieved and delighted to be back in the city which had been her home for five years; she picked up again on the dialect as if she'd never been away. She ran from room to room in the big house on New Lane, rejoicing both in what was different and what was reassuringly familiar. To her amazement, there was a small collection of parcels from her parents that had arrived after she had left – they had been carefully put to one side, anticipating her eventual return! She loved seeing 'her' children – how they'd grown, of course, and how in many cases they had matured spiritually. Pastor and Mrs Wang were overjoyed to see her again; the McCarthys had moved on to another station.

The Taylors were glad to change into the familiar padded Chinese garments as the bitter winter approached. Hudson then set off on his travels: there were personnel challenges among the missionaries in many of the stations, as well as sickness and even deaths. Chinese Christians were in some places suffering persecution; but still there was encouragement, with much church growth. Meanwhile, Jennie settled back into Hangchow life for a few weeks. Two additional teachers destined for Hangchow had travelled out with them to China; Jennie now concentrated on helping induct them into the schools. But she didn't herself pick up on the work in any way: her calling was now very different.

The Taylors spent Christmas at Hangchow; as warm memories flooded back, particularly for Jennie, they sat down to an ample festive spread provided by Hudson for members of the church. There were more celebrations over the New Year, including fun with a magic lantern show. And they also, for the first time since their wedding, managed to snatch a day or so alone together. Jennie was now blossoming out into the middle trimester of a healthy pregnancy; she was also loving being back in China in the company of her dear husband. But soon it was time to move on.

First, they returned by boat to Shanghai, then inland up the Yangtze as far as Nanking, one-time mighty capital of the Ming dynasty. They would be settling here for a while, at least until after the baby was born. Life was very different here, in this bustling city with its towering walls – but Jennie, as ever, was content to stay wherever they believed God placed them. Her husband had ongoing pastoral concerns about Charlie – maybe his underlying problem was simply an inability to settle without Nellie – but at the same time his administrative skills were such that Hudson didn't want to lose him, so he was brought along too. So, Nanking became effectively the Mission headquarters in China. The positive significance of this, Nanking having been the HQ of the violent Taipings, who were ravaging China when Hudson Taylor first arrived in 1854, was not lost on them. Jennie would be more in the heart of things now than she had ever been in Hangchow, in more ways than one.

Meanwhile, back in London things were tough for Emily. The Council of Management, while using the Pyrland Road premises as the address of the Mission, were not, of course, experiencing the immediacy of living there. Neither for that matter had any of them set foot in China. To make matters worse, there were signs that Richard Hill, still with secular business responsibilities, had bitten off more CIM responsibility than he could chew. It was the weakening Emily who remained the most vital link with China, and the one to deal with everyday issues such as correspondence and casual callers – as well as looking after the Taylor children. She remained cheerful, getting on brilliantly with the increasingly indispensable 'Ettie' Soltau, but deep down there was sadness, and she missed the Taylors sorely.

By January 1873 her letters to China were in pencil, so she could write lying down. But amazingly she kept on top of her secretarial duties, while Henrietta took over the running of the household. They each wrote to the Taylors, claiming it was the other who was working the harder.

Jennie found plenty she liked about Nanking. 'The air is more bracing', she told her parents. They wondered at her unceasing ability to find the best in everything. She enjoyed pleasant strolls along the city walls, and soon made friends, managing to make herself understood in the local dialect. She went to chapel for as long as she could, where 'good work' was taking place, including among 'Mohammedans'.

The sitting room where Jennie found she was resting more and more doubled as Hudson's study, with his desk in one corner – so she was content. She wrote home that she was in good hands. They had a good cook, and a 'help', and the cook kept a goat, so she was getting plenty of milk. 'We always have seemed to be happily circumstanced', she reflected. She also said that she would be well looked after throughout her confinement by Louise Desgraz, the last remaining single woman from the *Lammermuir* who was still within the Mission. There was always plenty of support from other CIM mothers, able to tell her what to expect. Sadly, too, there were always those around who had lost a baby.

She was keeping well, even beyond the time when Hudson said the baby would arrive. Early April came, warm with the promise of spring – but still no baby. Jennie was now beginning to tire easily.

Then on Saturday 12 April things started to happen. The regular pains started coming at around eight in the morning. But things did not progress as they should. A whole twenty-four hours passed, and still no sign of any baby. At dawn Hudson sent for another colleague with medical knowledge. Jennie could tell her strength was failing: fear was threatening to take hold. Finally at 1.30 p.m. on Sunday 13 April Jennie gave birth to a boy – but devastatingly, he had not survived. He had a potentially robust appearance and Hudson presumed he had been healthy at least up until the confinement had begun.

In the evening the medical colleague returned to check that all was well; the trauma of the day's events had not completely impacted Jennie, who was more comfortable, but hardly awake – when alarmingly the pains started rhythmically again. After examination, much to everyone's shock, Hudson announced there was another baby on the way! The little girl didn't arrive until the Monday evening – and sadly she too had died. She was in more of a sorry state than her brother, and Jennie blamed herself, suggesting the hard work of the last forty-eight hours had adversely affected her (although Hudson's opinion was that she had died on the Saturday, at around the same time as her brother).

Hudson wrote to the Fauldings with as much information as he felt they could bear. Knowing with relief that their daughter had survived, they coped with the lesser shock of the babies. As with all their letters from China, news coming after the event could give no cause for present alarm.

On 21 April, Jennie felt strong enough physically and emotionally to write to her parents for herself. She reported that she had been well looked after throughout by her husband, and by Louise Desgraz. All in all, it was not so much the pain as the exhaustion of such a protracted labour, she said. The pain in the second labour had been greatly eased by the use of the new wonder drug, chloroform. Typically, she expressed herself in terms of how the whole sad episode would leave others. But how her own heart ached, as she gazed round the room at the many packages sent from home, still lying unopened in anticipation of the glad event. She would have to find new homes now for items she had purchased or lovingly prepared for her baby. She now felt she knew for the first time something of the depths of the multiple losses felt by Maria and Hudson. No longer was she 'just' the onlooker; she was tasting something of sacrifice for herself.

Months later, Hudson was still suffering the devastation of the loss. Writing to Richard Hill concerning other losses on the field, he said 'I wonder what position our own little treasures so recently taken occupy among them'.

Fully expecting to have had a baby to look after in Nanking, grounding her in the work there for a while, Jennie now turned her thoughts to the fact she would at least be free to travel and visit with her husband. But she soon found constant itinerating unsettling; she wrote home that it was too tiring for her husband – but it was probably so for her also. Lingering tiredness from the disastrous

Her Calling Was Now Very Different (1872–74)   129

confinement, and in all probability anaemia also, sapped her normal enthusiasm for being by his side.

Then in the autumn of 1873 they received the telegram they had dreaded: the stark, doom-laden words ' . . . not expected [to] live many weeks she would like you to come' plunged them into a terrible quandary. For many reasons returning home was out of the question right now – but, in fact, Emily would survive for some months yet, and was still responsible for a prodigious amount of work. In the September someone ordered a waterbed for her. This new invention, for nursing the very sick, was growing in popularity in the United States, where Emily's bed was coming from; it was still virtually unknown in the UK.

At least the children were now thriving. The two oldest, Bertie (Herbert Hudson) and Freddie (Frederick Howard), were particularly bright boys, mastering all the usual subjects, and needing constant outlet for their enthusiasm and energy; Freddie was the livelier of the two, but 'Bertie also has a full share of conversational activity'. They handled Scripture with spiritual awareness – but a fairly typical level of naughtiness was apparent also. The Taylors were told such children, from strong Christian homes, often pass through a stage of 'very little difference from other children'!

Hudson wrote to Emily more often than Jennie did; his letters were full of spiritual intimacies, and of regret that he couldn't be there for her. This was entirely acceptable when it was understood that Emily was effectively mother to his four children, so in some ways part of his family. But the correspondence was also full of business matters. He couldn't help the fact that his trust in Emily, for both wisdom and efficiency, was greater than in the two 'Hon

Secs'. How different this was from the normal male-to-male business preferences of the time. He asked Emily to plead with Richard Hill not to make financial appeals – but they seemed slow in sending out funds when they were available; Emily would know that was part of the reason why the Taylors were currently unable to come home. In addition, Hudson would often mention his frequent headaches, and the fact he was so often almost beyond himself with the pressure of work on the field. Yet he deeply regretted burdening her also. All-in-all, a heady cocktail for Emily!

But there was also good news to convey: the Mission was constantly advancing further inland, baptising new converts and raising up Chinese church leaders; and always there were new recruits arriving from England.

In Nanking itself, where they were based, the church was now well established. Jennie was particularly pleased to report that Li Lanfeng, known to everyone at home, had arrived to pick up the pastorate.

By the spring of 1874, it was becoming a major preoccupation for the Taylors that they were so far from Emily, who was said to be dying, yet they were not free to leave. Jennie wrote expressing the hope that spring would bring an upturn in her friend's health. 'Can it be that Jesus is still sparing you for earth a little longer?' she said. The very dependable Louise Desgraz agreed to leave China and travel home to help relieve Emily – of both work and children.

Hudson was recognising his children were about to lose their second mother figure. He instructed that they should be sent to his parents for the time being. He still had work to do in China, and continued with the oversight which was so vital, yet which took so much out of him. Jennie was still tending to stay put, enjoying the pastoral work which came with being grounded in one church. But she wrote tirelessly to Hudson, and he leaned heavily on her wise and encouraging words.

The quandary continued: to go home or to stay; the two options constantly vied for supremacy in Hudson Taylor's mind and heart. But then came the shock event which forced his hand. He was on a Yangtze steamer aiming for Wuhan, many hundreds of miles upstream; the boat was so basic that it was deemed unsuitable for females. The ladders on board were narrow and vertical, and on 2 June he missed his footing, landing vertically and forcefully on his heels, severely jarring his spine. The pain was excruciating, and at first he was winded and unable to walk. There was then temporarily some improvement – but he was using crutches.

It was clear the invalid must go home.

13

The Mrs Taylor of the Party was Pregnant (1874–76)

With complex demands on Hudson Taylor's time, and with so much now needing to be delegated, it took a while for departure to be organised. Jennie wrote reassuringly to her parents, but a subsequent intense discussion was not so reassuring: Mrs Faulding's old worries were resurfacing concerning health issues in China. 'Is there never such a thing as people getting ill at home?' Jennie responded defensively. 'Mr Spurgeon is always having illnesses' – she selected her argument carefully; she knew they could hardly 'attribute [his problems] to climate'. Jennie's efforts at telling her mother not to worry often deteriorated into mild scolding; on one occasion she herself referred to 'this little sermon', saying to her mother 'you can either indulge or retrain your feelings [of worry]', and exhorting her to fill her time with good things 'which would help both you and others'.

The Taylors' passage was eventually booked for the August of 1874. And yet again, for the fourth time in Hudson's sailing experience, the Mrs Taylor of the party

The Mrs Taylor of the Party was Pregnant (1874–76) 133

was pregnant! Jennie was well enough, and looking forward to the tonic of time at sea, but her attitude to the pregnancy was understandably low-key.

They were travelling in the company of the Rudlands and family, well overdue a first furlough. The party was due in Dover on 14 October, but Mrs Rudland (Mary Bell of the *Lammermuir*) was so unwell in Paris that Jennie volunteered to stay there overnight with her, running the risk of leaving her parents temporarily disappointed at the dockside.

The Taylors knew, and deeply regretted, they would not be seeing Emily. Letters waiting for them in Marseilles told them she had in fact died before they had left – on 26 July. She had been laid to rest among the quiet leafy paths of the newly opened Highgate Cemetery East, yet to be made popular by the arrival of the remains of Karl Marx. With their hearts weighed down by grief, they made a point of visiting as soon as they were home. But the multiple assurances Emily had died at peace, fully anticipating her heavenly home, meant everything to them.

There were other changes too at Pyrland Road. For one it was rather quieter, now that Bertie and Freddie had at last gone to school. They had been enrolled, according to Hudson Taylor's wishes, in the prestigious City of London School. One of the Council of Management members, a trustee of Maria's legacy, had been specifically deputed to work on this, and make all the arrangements. (Jennie had increasingly become convinced she wanted all of her uncle's legacy, deposit and interest, to be used at her discretion for God's work in China or at home. In her case she chose not to reserve it for 'any children God may give us'. She was pregnant when she wrote these words. She instructed the trustees accordingly.)

The City of London School was founded in 1442 for 'the religious and virtuous education of boys'; it was currently situated in Milk Street, just off Cheapside in the City. The boys began in the spring term of 1874, when Herbert was coming up to 13, and Frederick still a boisterous 11. By the time they eventually left, the foundation stone had been laid on the much larger Thames Embankment site, where the school would still be situated more than 150 years later.

The faithful Louise Desgraz had arrived from China in the March of that year, in time to contribute to Emily's care at the end. Then after her death she moved into the newly acquired number 8, with the two younger Taylor children. This was just in time apparently, as an outbreak of scarlet fever descended just as the Taylors were arriving home. Everyone was either isolating or recovering.

Bertie, the first to succumb, was recuperating at his grandparents' in Barnsley. After their arrival, Jennie took Freddie, also missing school, with her to her parents, who after the disappointment of not moving out permanently to be near the Bergers in Sussex, were now living north of London, in rural Barnet. They were about to say goodbye to Nellie, sailing off at last to join her fiancé; they had to get used to feast or famine as far as seeing their daughters was concerned!

Altogether the two years since Hudson and Jennie had left for China had been a strange time of transition. The Bergers had sold Saint Hill, moving back to London but remaining involved. Their dear vicar friend Mr Pennefather had died in 1873, and sadly also Henrietta's sister Lucy. The ever-resourceful Henrietta herself, released from her care of Emily, had opened a home for missionaries' children on the south coast of England.

Hudson returned to his normal heavy workload; he was disappointed it was not the family reunion he had anticipated, but he was managing his injury well, and would soon be free of crutches. But then suddenly, almost overnight it seemed, instead of improvement pain and disability began to plague him once more: due to the inflammation in his spine his legs were virtually paralysed, and by December he was confined to bed. Family prayers, so recently reinstated after the scarlet fever, were now held in the bedroom, with Hudson listening carefully to the children's endless probing questions, pent up since his return from China. Charles particularly was now taking over from Bertie with his 'full share of conversational activity'.

The incessant work continued. Interviews, prayer meetings, dictation . . . even the Council was convened in his bedroom. And without Emily the workload was greater: he asked his mother if she would be good enough to edit the latest *Occasional Paper*.

Jennie helped Hudson to devise a rope mechanism above the bed to aid his sitting up and turning. They also hung a map of China at the foot of the bed. Seeing her husband so helpless, she expressed to others her fear that they would never now return to China. Indeed, to some it seemed the CIM itself was about to expire. What was happening to that sense of destiny they had felt so strongly in both their hearts? Certainly it would be impossible right now for him to go, and no one, least of all Hudson, would ever expect her to leave her husband's side and go on her own.

Just a week or so before Christmas, Hudson's problems increased, with an attack of his 'old' dysentery. Louise Desgraz came to look after him until his mother arrived from Barnsley, freeing Jennie to keep her distance, the baby being almost due. Young Maria and Charles were sent to stay with the Broomhall cousins in Godalming – although Amelia now had nine of her own.

Jennie's pregnancy this time round had been infinitely easier. In China, expecting undiagnosed twins, she was exhausted and virtually immobile at the end; now, looking back, she realised it had hardly been a template for future experience. The greater ease carried through into labour – and a rather precipitate delivery.

On 7 January 1875, there was an early morning prayer meeting round Hudson's bed. Jennie was resting, as was thought, in the room next door; but, in fact, her labour pains had begun. Anticipating plenty of time, she raised no alarm – but when eventually Louise Desgraz came to check on her, Ernest Hamilton Taylor had already arrived, small, but very much alive! Hudson was placed onto a moveable couch, and wheeled next door to cut the cord and do whatever else was necessary. They shared a few precious moments of joy and exhaustion together, then Hudson was wheeled back to bed.

Due partly, it was thought, to the 'fomentations' Hudson had suggested be applied to his back, the rest of January showed a gradual improvement; by the end of the month, he could walk unsupported into the next room. Nevertheless, he asked Louise to write to his parents on his behalf. She explained that due to ongoing disability he would still be unable to see them for a while. By way of explanation Louise told them the relapse had been due to 'overworking and twisting about in bed'!

By March he was in his study, with a couch nearby if needed. Not for the last time the builders were in at Pyrland Road, creating noise and dust while they knocked a doorway through between numbers 4 and 6. Jennie took baby Ernest and stayed for a while with the proud first-time grandparents in Barnet. A letter from Hudson arrived almost daily while she was there: as well as expressions of how much he missed his new little family he had plenty of medical advice for the new mother, such as when to give the castor oil, and a reminder to suck peppermint lozenges when 'nursing' the baby. Mother and baby responded well to each other; she was relieved he was not on the whole fretful or sickly, no doubt in part a result of her calm handling – but he did develop thrush in Barnet.

Jennie's brother, William, had recently married, and settled in Marylebone, so Mrs Faulding was also spending time helping them in their new home. William and Louisa eventually had six children.

Meanwhile on 6 February in Shanghai, Nellie and Charlie were married at last.

Hudson saw something in Henry Soltau which he particularly wanted to encourage – in fact, he had been begging him to come to China since before the formation of the Council. The strength of Hudson's conviction that no finances should ever be solicited was well matched at times by the pressure he could apply to people he thought should be in China.

Mr Soltau did eventually respond to what he felt was an irrevocable call from God. Leaving his professional work, and his half of the joint role of honorary secretary, he eventually set out across the globe. In order to reach the remote regions of south-west China he and a companion bravely faced the challenges of entering the country via 'Burmah'.

In a separate development, Hudson Taylor and others were now praying specifically for 'eighteen'. There remained nine as yet unreached provinces, each as large as a European country; with no Protestant missionary among them, Hudson wanted two single men to be sent to each province. As the need was publicised, Hudson set the bar high: this would be difficult, ground-breaking work, and as well as exemplary Christian character, a true pioneering spirit would be required.

At the same time, he was beginning to change some of his policies; he was asking now for a higher standard of education than had been found among the artisans of the *Lammermuir*; he drafted a standard application form, including a question on willingness to self-fund during a period of probation. On marriage he was starting to think it better if couples waited two years after arriving in China before marrying, seeing that period also as a time of probation. Hudson had certainly modified his once strongly held opinion that as soon as the intended life partner had been chosen, then to be married was in every way preferable to remaining unmarried.

The news from China was increasingly encouraging: the Yangchow riots seem to have been forgotten in China/UK relations, and it appeared safe to travel again. Also, the young opium-smoking, brothel-visiting Emperor Tong Zhi had just died, and this was thought to be good news, with the country more favourably governed as a result. No one was alarmed at the time by the fact the Dowager Empress Ci Xi was increasingly coming to the fore. When twenty men came forward in response to the call for the Eighteen, as they became known, it was all a tonic to Hudson – and an encouragement therefore to Jennie.

It was at around this time that the well-known Guinness family began to enter the CIM story. Grattan Guinness, whom Taylor had first met in Dublin, was opening a missionary training college in the East End of London. Harley College, as it was called, was situated on the Bow Road near the Taylors' previous home in Coborn Street. He wanted his students to receive practical work experience among London's most needy, and for this he started linking in with Dr Barnardo. He was soon feeding many of his capable young graduates into the CIM also. And when in the years to come a Taylor eventually married a Guinness, their lives would be permanently interwoven.

By the end of April, Hudson was managing stairs unaided. As the weather grew warmer, he was spending time praying or dictating in the garden. Jennie watched the gradual return to previous levels of activity with mixed feelings: as much as her heart was for the work in China, she was tempted at times to fear her husband would set off before he was truly fit.

For years Hudson had intermittently asked Amelia and Benjamin Broomhall to consider going to China. Now he was beginning to formulate a different plan, one with which they were perhaps more likely to agree. Would they consider moving to Pyrland Road – even perhaps for an experimental period?

Benjamin's drapery business was in trouble, with possible bankruptcy looming. They had been in leafy Godalming, from where Benjamin had commuted to his business in London, for just four years, but with reduced income they were going to have to move again. Hudson knew the combined skills of this couple would be exactly what the home base needed, to put it on an efficient footing at last. He was also now seriously thinking himself of a return to China, to work with the Eighteen as they begin to settle in. An overhaul in the home team would be even more important.

As well as an administrator, Benjamin was a publicist; he had already worked tirelessly on behalf of the abolition both of slavery, and the opium trade. He could speak eloquently on any subject dear to his heart, and would be a brilliant advocate for the Mission. Amelia, on the other hand, was a highly organised homemaker, and having servants just increased her homely leadership skills. Her caring nature would undoubtedly extend to welcoming and settling any female candidates. This radical change in circumstances would involve a more-than-full-time role for each of them, as well as demanding their total spiritual dedication. The Broomhalls moved into 2 Pyrland Road in the August of 1875 – and stayed for forty years!

Jennie decided this was exactly the kind of use to which she wished her money to be put. She was delighted it would help to support the Broomhalls, and their now ten children.

Meanwhile, one or two of the Eighteen were beginning to depart for the East. More than a thousand gathered at Mr Spurgeon's enormous Metropolitan Tabernacle to give a rousing send-off to the first contingent. Another farewell service was held in Dr Barnardo's Edinburgh Castle in the

East End of London – a converted gin palace, now a mission hall and a workers' coffee house.

In the midst of everything else, Hudson and his Council were discussing a major change in their means of publicising the work. *Occasional Papers* were good – but something of perhaps wider appeal and popular challenge was needed, with the message encapsulated somehow in its title. He discussed this at length with Jennie also, and she put forward *China's Millions and our work among them*. This met with instant unanimous approval. The first edition came out in the July (1875), and was monthly from then on. The banner headline was *China's Millions* from the start; *and our work among them* appeared underneath in smaller lettering. But from the following January it was simply *China's Millions*. This remained its name for seventy-seven years – and after almost 150 years, a variation of the name was still being employed. With this, if with nothing else, Jennie had left her indelible mark on the Mission.

It was thought at the time the *Occasional Paper* would continue, at roughly half-yearly intervals, but as it turned out issue number 39, published in the March of the same year, proved to be the last.

China's Millions represented a massive conceptual change, from a small-format, small-print 'need-to-know' pamphlet to a more presentation style, intended to draw interest and to match the expanding work, which needed greater prayerful and financial support. From the start there was a young readers' column, and in each of the early months there was a sample from Emily Blatchley's spiritually profound poetic compositions. But the most striking innovation was the fact it was illustrated. From the very first edition there were beautiful woodcut engravings of Chinese scenes, courtesy of *The Graphic* magazine, a recent rival to *The Illustrated London News*. Then photos started appearing, courtesy of *Illustrations of China and its People* by John Thomson. The pictures increased the costs considerably, but all were encouraged as circulation also increased month on month as the issues came out: it looked as if financially they might eventually break even.

In the August, by way of celebration after completion of the first edition, Hudson and Jennie took their family to Guernsey for a rare summer break.

Jennie was pregnant again by the autumn, and feeling much more sanguine than previously. She wrote to Louise Desgraz, who was returning to China. They had only just noticed, Jennie wrote, that with the production each month of *China's Millions* no one had had time to produce another *Occasional Paper*.

Jennie thanked Louise for the clock she had left her. She was finding it invaluable: 'it calls me and I call the servants at 5.30 every morning'.

In the January of 1876, Richard Hill wrote to Hudson Taylor suggesting Henry Soltau's brother William as the replacement secretary to the Mission – but full-time, not honorary. He was both willing and suitable, and after all, Mr Taylor must be relieved 'of the burdensome routine of the Home work of the Mission'. This was a cry from the heart of the willing but overworked Mr Hill. William would be the sixth from a possible nine Soltau siblings to be committed to the China Inland Mission. In the end he was the replacement treasurer, invaluable alongside the already well-settled Benjamin Broomhall.

The Mrs Taylor of the Party was Pregnant (1874–76)

Also in the January, Jennie had news that Nellie in Shanghai had survived cholera, then safely given birth to her first baby. She would go on to have nine more.

It would not be long before Jennie's own baby was due. As the final weeks approached, she told Louise that she felt stronger than she had done in the comparable period before Ernest was born. She could allow herself to be more confident this time round. She also had wonderful support from the new neighbours: the Broomhalls at number 2 were a great blessing, especially where help with the children was concerned. She had recently had to let the mother's help go: Hudson had observed that she had a way of upsetting Charlie and Ernie, and 'things were not working out'. But there was a new servant, who was hard-working, and Jennie was grateful for the extra pair of hands – although in a letter she complained she 'lacks brains'.

Into this brief period of settled domesticity, Amy Hudson Taylor made her appearance, on 17 April 1876.

14

Moving Forward at an Incredible Rate (1876–78)

With restored health and a good home team, Hudson was now anxious to be back in China. Planning a short visit of perhaps nine or ten months, he set off in September 1876.

Just for a while, Jennie was glad to be staying put. In a few weeks, with Amy more established, perhaps she and the two children would join Hudson in China, coping in much the same way as Maria had done. The older four, of course, would be better off at home.

As it happened, her sister and brother-in-law had had to return home that autumn, for the sake of Charlie's health. Due to the fact they both had access to private incomes (Nellie's similar to Jennie's), they were able to set up in a large house in Colvestone Crescent, barely a mile from Pyrland Road. Here they were able to rest and recover, and establish their eventually very large family. Charles Fishe joined the Home Council when he was better until, nineteen years later, they returned to China. Jennie enjoyed being 'round the corner' from her sister for a while. The Fauldings were not about to complain, either.

Moving Forward at an Incredible Rate (1876–78)

Soon after reaching China, Hudson Taylor found he had to conduct a funeral. Catherine Stronach had arrived in China in 1868, and had married George Duncan, one of the original *Lammermuir* party. They had one little daughter, Mary, but sadly George died in 1873. Catherine continued on bravely as a single parent in China, subsequently marrying William Stronach in the February of 1876 – but tragically she then died also, just nine months later.

She had had one dying wish, that if at all possible Mary (always known as Millie) would be brought up alongside the Taylors' own children. The plan was that she would be taken back to London by her stepfather, where Jennie, and sixteen lively Broomhall and Taylor children, would be ready to welcome her.

With the 'adoption' of Millie Duncan, Hudson and Jennie's family of seven children would be complete. Of the seven, it was only Amy who never set foot in China.

Once more separation from each other produced a cascade of mail. Hudson always included 'love and kisses' to his four older children and, somewhat persistently, to 'Ernie and baby'. Almost daily he poured out in his letters his love for Jennie. And if she ever doubted it: 'It is not for want of love for you that I have left England.' They also wrote to each other extensively in Romanised Chinese.

He sent love to Jennie's parents, continuing to maintain a warm relationship with Mrs Faulding, and commenting 'I was touched by her kindness – I think she has forgiven me' – presumably for the precipitate way in which he married their daughter!

With Hudson away the Council, including William Soltau, and Benjamin at the helm, was back in vicarious charge. Yet Jennie was the one who had the intimate knowledge of China. As with Emily, it was easier sometimes for Hudson just to bypass the Council, so with every love letter came plenty of directives. Jennie understood the cryptic language sometimes required, in case letters fell into the wrong hands: the smallest perceived slight on the Chinese could lead to a diplomatic incident.

Whenever Hudson dreamt of Jennie, he would be sure to mention it, plus the pain of waking up afterwards. Invariably also he would comment as to deficiencies in his health, or major personnel or other concerns which as he often said, were stretching him almost beyond endurance; this wasn't easy for Jennie, caring about him so much, but feeling so helpless.

Much of *China's Millions* was now being constructed remotely; each edition was sent to Hudson for his final edit. There was an important communication to be included in the February 1877 edition – the news from the home front that the very dear Mary Berger had passed away. The entire CIM family, on whichever side of the globe they were, felt they were mourning the loss of a personal friend.

Increasingly, Hudson recognised the importance of articles with popular appeal: descriptions of everyday life in China, of the shopkeeper or the farmer, for instance, always with a beautiful woodcut to illustrate.

By Christmas he was writing from Chinkiang, a city on the Yangtze with which they were both familiar. Progress into the nine 'new' provinces was moving forward at an incredible rate, partly due to the signing of the Chefoo Convention in September 1876, the month he had left home. This convention insured, among other things, that with a passport a foreigner could travel freely and safely throughout China. With characteristic urgency, the CIM were maximising their opportunity to move inland.

At home, Jennie was bonding well with the four oldest children; Charlie had started calling her Mamma. The Fauldings had taken to them also. With no Saint Hill, and no Godalming, 273 Lyonsdown Road, Barnet was now their country retreat. Jennie had not lost her teenage ability to move easily between her parents' comfortable and genteel surroundings, and the rough-and-ready Taylor residence, now her own home. She was anxious to save her parents having to do the same thing, and perhaps catching sight of bare floorboards or a cold hearth. They were relieved about one aspect of life at Pyrland Road, however. All the CIM houses were rented, but before he left, Hudson had made a rare if gentle financial appeal for help to buy them outright. The opportunity, if taken, would save the Mission vast sums in rent.

But news about the 60-year-old Mrs Faulding's health was not so good: according to the doctor, her heart was weakening.

The weeks stretched to months. Jennie was clearly needed as a valuable member of the home team, so was hardly free to join her husband. Before he returned to the UK, he had an important international gathering to attend: originally proposed by the Presbyterians, the first 'General Conference for Missionaries in China' was taking place in the May of 1877 in Shanghai. The 126 delegates present, male and female, represented twenty different Protestant missionary societies – a small gathering compared with those of the future, but vital nevertheless in discussing the varying approaches to mission, of all societies represented. The group photo, reproduced in *China's Millions*, showed a tiny minority of missionaries in Chinese dress – all members of the CIM!

Jennie, meanwhile, had a distraction at home which drew her interest.

Catherine Pennefather, widow of their fondly remembered vicar friend, had a project of her own. As a couple, as well as their vanguard of spiritual leadership, the Pennefathers had long had a social conscience; their enterprising training school for deaconesses equipped middle-class Christian young ladies, desperate to escape lives of leisure and do something worthwhile, to work in some of the most deprived areas of East London. (Two of the *Lammermuir* ladies – two of the three who were baptised at Anjer – had been trained by the Pennefathers.) Now, since her husband's death, with his memorial fund at her disposal, Mrs Pennefather decided to found a mission hospital in Bethnal Green, one of the areas in which the deaconesses were active.

The Mildmay Mission Hospital, as it was called, was opened in 1877; it started with a male, a female and a children's ward. Opening Day was an event not to be missed, by all their many supporters in London and beyond, including all the residents of the CIM's houses in Pyrland Road.

The 'Mildmay' would still have its vital place on the London medical scene well into the twenty-first century.

Hudson was finally free to leave China at the end of October. The Taylors had been apart already for an unthinkable thirteen months.

Moving Forward at an Incredible Rate (1876–78) 149

By the time he was almost home in early December, his mind was on whether even Ernest would remember him; he knew Amy wouldn't. He was worrying too about the challenge of a probable very public reunion with his wife. On dockside, station platform, even the steps of Pyrland Road . . . how would they handle it, after so long? Would self-consciousness spoil the very moment they were now both living for?

Jennie, for her part, allowed herself to be excited. With Hudson home in time for Christmas, she would make sure it was a good one – as restful as possible for him, with now seven lively youngsters. With candidates leaving for China at frequent intervals, and things going well when they got there, she imagined they would be based at home for a while. Certainly there was always more than enough to be done, even with Benjamin Broomhall so ably taking up the reins. Benjamin was already itinerating, enjoying hosting meetings in Birmingham, warming to his passionate theme, of God's work in China. Well-spoken, and dapper in appearance, he was also comfortable addressing the titled and wealthy among CIM's London friends.

It was just before leaving China that Hudson received the dark news. He was contacted by the London Missionary Society (LMS) in Peking, who told him about the severe famine raging in Shansi (not to be confused with Shensi) province. Then he heard similar news from his CIM colleagues: other provinces were affected, but things were deteriorating rapidly in Shansi, beyond the power of the Chinese authorities to cope. The Catholics were already raising funds, we must do the same, said the CIM missionaries. The LMS suggested to Hudson that he specifically send his men to spend the winter there, anticipating the famine would last at least until the spring.

Jennie too had heard about Shansi. The awful fact of the famine hung over them like the presence of a silent and unacknowledged guest for Christmas. They celebrated being 'family' again, however, Hudson enjoying reacquaintance with Ernest and Amy. Bertie announced he now wished to be called Herbert. Now almost 17, he was anticipating medical training. Freddie too would soon be known as 'Howard', his middle name. Maria, at 11, was now taking 8-year-old Millie to school.

Most of Shansi's 16 million people lived on the normally fertile Great Plain of Taiyuen (the capital of Shansi). In good times it is watered by the River Fen, flowing from the north down through the capital. But these were not good times. There had been no rain, and no crops to speak of, for three years. There was no grass for animals, just clouds of the sandy soil being blown across the plains; even the emperor's Forbidden City in Peking, hundreds of miles away, was receiving a light dusting of yellow. The missionaries who had already advanced through Shansi had commented on unspeakable deprivations in the population. Beggars, usually women and children, would wander in groups, holding out bowls pitifully if they encountered anyone. Others approached offering to sell their daughters. As often happens in times of famine, there was always some food, but at vastly inflated prices, such that the wealthy exploited the situation. Millions were starving, possibly a third of the Shansi population. Some refugees did make it as far as Tientsin, a city on the coast – but died there of disease in appalling overcrowding. Worst of all, cannibalism had been reported.

Hudson set to with publicity and fundraising. Donations were soon coming in specifically for famine relief as opposed to mission work. The missionaries on the ground there were beginning to encounter the orphans of the famine, also extraordinary numbers of 'unwanted' females. They were doing their best to offer them shelter. Hudson suggested to Louise Desgraz, working hard in the South, that perhaps she could expand the capacity of their boarding schools. But how would they get the orphans there?

The nation as a whole eventually responded. The Archbishop of Canterbury and the Lord Mayor of London got involved, and in February 1878, The China Famine Relief Committee was formed to coordinate a national response.

And eventually, true to type, the Taylors felt things personally. It was never enough just to send others, sitting comfortably at home themselves. But Hudson was not fully fit, and having just returned he was immersed in the demands at home. Their youngest were tiny. It was not a good time to go. But the situation was difficult to push from their minds.

It was the age-old quandary for missionaries – is there ever a right time to put the needs of a suffering world before their own children? Hudson had once written from China that he felt ashamed that '[Jennie] and the dear children should affect me so much more than millions here perishing'. At such times guilt lay crouching at the door – a powerful emotion that could work in either direction.

As spring approached, and the famine was still rife, news began to come through of some coordination; missionaries were beginning to gather in Taiyuen, and strategies were emerging particularly in south-east Shansi, in and around the capital; J.J. Turner, one of CIM's 'Eighteen', was among the first to arrive. A centre was set up, from where relief could be distributed. But orphanages were required as well as food.

What was really needed, everyone was beginning to realise, was a team of women, able to work with the 'unwanted' children, and to start orphanage and schools work; their leader must be an experienced and capable female, courageous, with a strong constitution, fluent in Chinese, mature and respected by the men of other missions. Who on earth should it be?

In March Hudson came up with the answer – before Jennie did.

Her days of adventure were past; it had never occurred to her for a moment that she should ever have to set off for China again on her own. She was certainly not drawn to the idea of abandoning her husband; this enterprise had to be from God, or completely foolhardy. The possibility started to be discussed openly, and gradually Jennie began to think that perhaps it really was God's will that she should leave husband and family behind, with the exception of Amy, and go to China. It might not be for long of course, as Hudson would soon find his way to join her, possibly bringing Ernest, when he was fully fit.

She had one or two detractors, however, the obvious point being about the irresponsibility of leaving her young son at this time. The arguments were compelling, so she did something she'd never done before – she 'put down a fleece' – she was going to put God to the test.

She asked God for a specific sum of money to be given her for her own and Amy's needs for the journey. She asked at the prayer meeting for others to join her in this petition, not of course mentioning what exactly her request to God was. She felt, if God answered this particular prayer, it would assure her that their other needs would be met, and it was indeed in obedience to God, not just her husband, that she was going.

Although a sizeable gift, the money arrived in full – from Hudson's (unknowing) parents.

By 12 April, Jennie was absolutely certain she was meant to be going. Ernie and Millie would go with the four older children to live with the Broomhalls, along with Jane, Jennie's latest hired 'help'.

Amelia Broomhall was quite amazing in her many skills. Motherly yet highly organised, she saw it as her life's calling to put home and family first – and to be at the service of one such as Jennie, who was obeying a calling of a different kind. This was the least she could do, she felt, as she and Benjamin had resisted Hudson's repeated call to go to China. All the cousins blended well, in age and interests. It was a testimony to the two very different sets of parents that five out of the ten Broomhalls and four out of the seven Taylors eventually went to the mission field.

Thanking Hudson's parents for their timely gift, albeit given in ignorance, Jennie wrote: 'I feel cast upon God, but He will not fail us. It is a serious undertaking.' Her own parents voiced uncertainty at first – but were getting to be beyond shock.

Up until 24 April Jennie was taking 2-year-old Amy – until she developed whooping cough at the last minute. A life-threatening disease, this added a still deeper dimension to Jennie's need to trust God completely that leaving now was the right thing.

In the days leading up to departure there were some huge farewell meetings. These included one at Spurgeon's Metropolitan Tabernacle, another hosted by Mr Guinness at his East London Institute – and one at Wesley's Chapel in the City Road at which a certain Revd William Faulding, Jennie's newly ordained brother, spoke.

Then the day before she boarded, £1,000 was given her for an orphanage in the famine-afflicted area.

On 2 May 1878 Jennie began her journey to China, with her team of two females; with two others they met up with in Shanghai, Jennie would lead the first party of western women ever to venture into China's interior. She was about to prove herself a true pioneer.

15

The Dead and Dying Lay Everywhere (1878–79)

The sight of a mass migration of people in times of flood, famine or plague is as old as China itself. Even so, some said the Northern Chinese Famine was the worst the world had ever known.

The challenge facing Jennie was enormous. During the voyage she dwelt on God's faithfulness to her thus far; she felt the whole enterprise would only be possible if she trusted God to lead her one small step at a time. At first it was thought there would be plenty for her to do with refugees arriving in the Yangtze region.

Meanwhile, at each port during the journey Jennie received updates from Hudson concerning the children. When she had left, all seventeen children had been divided between home, and the Taylor grandparents now in Hastings, depending on whether or not they were currently suffering from whooping cough. But Amy was now 'exceedingly well' and Jane the nurse was a 'bright and happy girl'. Jennie thanked her in-laws for looking after 'our dear chicks' even when they were poorly. When they were all back in London it was decided Jane would take Ernest, Amy and Millie to Barnet. Far from missing out on their grandchildren, the Fauldings continued to fulfil their fair share of childcare; the hayfield at the bottom of their garden was a wonderful bonus in that regard.

Hudson was also able to assure Jennie that her mother was now exceedingly proud of her; the Fauldings, at great personal cost, had come a long way.

Jennie reached Shanghai in June; Celia Horne and Anna Crickmay, two single ladies who had already been in China for two years, were the two who joined her team there. Some two hundred famine orphans were already in the region and in need of housing, and Jennie's first job was to establish orphanages for them in CIM premises. At first, she had much travelling to do, back and forth to various CIM stations, including to Nanking. But then there appeared to be a change of policy. Removing vulnerable victims from the famine region was not such a good idea after all.

For a start, as soon as they reached the South, many females and orphans were quickly sold on, before the CIM could house them. It was true that the best hope for some women might be to be taken in and employed by wealthy southern households, but that kind of advantageous arrangement was not exactly what most would have waiting for them!

Additionally, it was realised it would be better if the powers that be in the famine region could see their orphans were actually being well looked after, not stolen. The whole relief enterprise had come under suspicion to start with. It was important not to give the Chinese any excuse to wonder what the 'foreign devils' were getting up to now.

Jennie started to receive advice from some of the leading missionaries active in Shansi. The LMS, based in Peking, but increasingly having a handle on the crisis (the ones who had originally alerted Hudson to the famine), wrote to Jennie advising her she was needed in Taiyuen. She had contact also with Revd Timothy Richard of the Baptist Missionary Society (BMS). He had been based in the coastal province of Shantung (which had suffered the beginnings of the famine the year before) but he was now in Taiyuen and, with his previous famine experience, was key to the whole operation. At about the same time she heard from Hudson, writing in similar vein. His information told him also that she should make her way to Taiyuen, the heart of the famine.

But then in Nanking there was an unexpected setback: Jennie contracted cholera. This was the last place she needed to be, in which to succumb to a possibly life-threatening condition: Nanking provoked harrowing memories of her tragic confinement there. Her underlying health profile was good, however, and she quickly fought back and recovered.

She began to prepare her team for the long and uncomfortable journey to Taiyuen. First, they steamed up the coast to the port of Tientsin; then on 21 September 1878, they set out on the arduous journey inland to Shansi. After months leading up to this moment it was with mixed emotions Jennie was finally able to write: 'And now we are on our way.'

To add to the challenge, she was travelling to an area that was so different from her previous experience of China, it might as well be a new country.

The northern Chinese ate, slept and travelled differently from the people of the South. Even the shape of their windows was different, Jennie commented in a letter home. Her one-time spirit of adventure was briefly rekindled on her first sighting of a caravan of camels: forty or fifty huge double-humped Bactrians in a long line as far as the eye could see, which on closer inspection revealed some of the people driving them looked different also. But mostly travel was by springless cart or mule litter, or the ubiquitous wheelbarrow, with sail attached to assist over the longer distances, but still just one wheel. There were certainly no canals for an easy ride. Sedan chairs, a popular means of transport in cultured Hangchow, were also a rare sight in Shansi.

The people of the region were more used to dealing with flooding than with drought. The *Hwang Ho*, or Yellow River, had a habit of overflowing its banks, giving rise to what was known as China's Sorrow. Shansi itself, about the size of England and Scotland together, is flanked to the south and the west by the Yellow River; to the east lies a mountain range, to be traversed by Jennie's party, and to the north there is the Great Wall (another source of fascination to Jennie). The light sandy soil, the *loess* of the central plain, was potentially fertile: with good rain it could yield two harvest seasons a year. In better times the inhabitants of this somewhat enclosed province were a self-sufficient and prosperous people. But in all the differences, Jennie was as quick as ever to identify the positives. She tuned in quickly to the different accents and dialects, and was soon reporting that she liked the Shansi temperament.

In the early stages of their journey there was little sign of famine, although food was becoming increasingly expensive as they approached the famine-stricken area. In fact, Jennie's descriptions for her mother were at this stage generally favourable. They were enjoying stunning scenery, sunny weather and no mud!

The covered two-wheeled carts in which they travelled were pulled by one mule, with the spare trotting alongside. The combination of lack of suspension and unforgiving rutted tracks meant it was best to sit on as much bedding as possible; walking for a while was also an option. As they bumped along for hour after hour, Jennie's one regret was she couldn't read, although she did confess in correspondence later that one could hardly think either.

At night in the villages the mules found the inn almost by instinct. The travellers sat down to bowls of noodles, not the rice dishes they would have had in the South, after which they settled to their night's sleep on the typical raised brick platforms known as *kangs*, which were heated in winter.

Twice they had to cross a river: the carts, baggage and presumably passengers were secured on barges; the mules had to swim. Eventually they were in the mountains. The rutted tracks became narrower and steeper; the mode of transport had to change to mule litter – one long narrow 'bed', just wide enough for two, and long enough to lie down, slung between two mules, one leading, one bringing up the rear. Unusually for Jennie, she was suddenly conscious of the fearful remoteness of the region. But as ever she was positive, full of gratitude to God for this great privilege that was hers.

They arrived in Taiyuen on 23 October – 'a part of China where a foreign woman has never been seen' Jennie was quoted in *China's Millions*.

On arrival, they found CIM's Mr Turner dangerously ill. He was nursed back to recovery mainly by David Hill of the Wesleyan Methodists. With Timothy Richard of the BMS this inter-denominational trio were the leaders of the local relief effort. They keenly anticipated the arrival of Mrs Taylor and her team, welcoming them as the missing links in their vital life-saving network. Although it was neither BMS nor Methodist policy, all three leaders, Hill, Richard and, of course, Turner, wore Chinese garb throughout their time in Taiyuen.

It wasn't long before Jennie and her team of ladies, on venturing out to the villages, were confronted with a succession of the most terrible of scenes. The dead and dying lay everywhere. If there was strength left at all, today's survivors would throw yesterday's victims into the communal pit. Homes had been dismantled, either in a desperate bid to raise a few 'cash' (a 'cash' was a low-value copper coin) from the materials, or more likely to salvage anything edible like the sorghum stalks from the roofing. Trees were stripped bare of leaves and even bark, anything that could be boiled down to eat. All domestic animals and beasts of burden long since consumed, adults were turning to selling their children; and cannibalism, the ultimate degradation, was taking place. Wild animals were equally hungry: vultures continually hovered, while crazed wolves were now attacking openly in the streets. The sights, the deathly smells, the spine-chilling moans and lamentations, a challenge to any well-bred Victorian lady, were now alas commonplace.

In the November, Jennie reassured her parents they were able themselves to access food, albeit at a price. Also by the November they had purchased their first premises for an orphanage – dilapidated, but under Jennie's supervision soon in reasonable shape. The donations from home towards the cost of orphanages were quickly disappearing. Four hundred children were receiving relief in Taiyuen.

Basic food supplies were starting to arrive in the region. The Chinese government, who provided the equivalent of 2 million pounds-worth of aid, were responsible for bringing grain from the plenteous South – from hundreds of miles inland up the Yangtze. When money needed transporting, magistrates always supplied armed escorts. Strings of copper 'cash' were heavy, so lumps of silver were often used for large amounts. When needed, the appropriate amount was shaved off and weighed.

Meanwhile, Timothy Richard coordinated funds from the UK Famine Relief Committee; this was distributed amongst all active missions, Protestant and Catholic. Grain was purchased, and distributed tightly and systematically, family by family, village by village, twenty or so villages to each distribution point. The worst-affected villages were visited personally, with a basin of millet provided for each home as immediate relief.

Before such detailed organisation, mob violence was a real threat; all those involved grew in practical wisdom, but it was Mr Richard's observation from the biblical 'Feeding of the Five Thousand' – that Jesus didn't distribute the food until everyone was sitting down – which transformed some distribution: the mob are less inclined to riot when sitting down.

Jennie explained in her update in *China's Millions* that not all the money donated would go directly for food for the dying or immediately destitute. Planning had to be for realistic and long-term rehabilitation; rains had begun to come again, but of course the next harvest had not even been sown. Even when the worst might be over the repercussions would continue. The CIM and other societies had to plead for giving at home to be sustained.

As food became available, money or coupons were often distributed. Again this could be invidious, with younger males able to push forward at distribution points. So, the policy became not to disclose how much would be given out on each occasion. In an imaginative reinterpretation of the biblical story of the hired servants, the stronger, more assertive males were encouraged to come forward first, disappearing almost immediately to cash their coupons in. The women, often representing family needs, then came forward, and were given up to four times as much!

And all the time 'orphans' were turning up, sometimes alone, but often there were parents demanding payment in exchange. More buildings were constantly needed, and the authorities were allocating redundant temples for Mission use.

The destitute always arrived with next to no clothing, all having been previously sold; Jennie therefore organised sewing groups for able women. With funds available she could pay them, enabling them to obtain the price-inflated food for themselves. The tightrope of exactly how to help people was always a challenge. 'By giving work to all who will do it we shall . . . not pauperise the people', Jennie explained. But direct charity could not always be avoided. The famine was still presenting itself in varying degrees of severity. Even when it was thought the worst was over, desperate skeletal individuals were still occasionally turning up on Mission doorsteps, reporting that in their entire family, they alone had survived.

Some villages were empty ghost villages – but if any did survive, they would inevitably be among the youngest, strongest and wealthiest – which better enabled the long, slow climb back to a semblance of normality.

Then in the December (of 1878), still in the worst of times and now with the northern snows, Jennie had a letter from Amelia. The update was vital, but nevertheless highlighted her remoteness from her children and the home base. In the letter Amelia reported that Amy now called her 'Mamma'. Ernie, however, now more 'boy-like', called her 'Auntie', and knew his mamma was in China. Millie, the last child to have caught whooping cough, was inclined to be clingy; Hudson was currently dosing her with cod liver oil.

With mixed feelings, Jennie wrote to her sister Nellie, pouring out her longing for home and family: 'But I have never for a moment regretted coming to China.' Her time was full, she reported, with orphanages, visiting and sewing classes. She said Mr Richard, and the new Mrs Richard, had earned her enormous respect.

Other news from home disclosed that Hudson's health was still a cause for concern. Some wealthy friends had arranged a holiday for him in Switzerland, so in the August he had been shipped off to the Continent for a month's rest cure. In Paris he still had headaches, but his cough was so much better that he was able to get out and about, enjoying the use of his 'Baedeker' guide. From there he had been taken to stay in the Swiss Alps, where his first-ever visit to a glacier did him a power of good. He had returned to London much improved.

Through all their separation, the Taylors' correspondence continued. A large proportion of Hudson's letters was given over to his outpourings of tender love and, of course, expressions of how much he missed Jennie. He unfailingly updated her on his poor state of health also (in the autumn he had believed 'his' malaria was returning spasmodically). By the time they were finally reunited it could be said that overall, and cholera notwithstanding, Jennie had enjoyed far better health, in their year of separation, than her husband.

In all it was thought 7 or 8 million people had died of famine or disease across the whole of northern China, half of that number being within Shansi. There were no children left in the region, other than those who had been taken to orphanages. Mission work saved maybe a quarter of a million lives – and permanently revolutionised attitudes to their presence. The tide of Chinese opinion had changed, meaning more work could be permanently established in the region; certainly there was a new open door in Shansi. In the midst of things, it had not been easy to give time to evangelism, but Mr Richard produced some posters calling on people to pray to the one true God, together with leaflets setting out the physical, political and religious causes of the famine, as he understood them – and the solutions. There was a new unity amongst the many missions and denominations, and for a while in Taiyuen they worshipped together.

In wider repercussions, Timothy Richard was acknowledged for his unique contribution by Lord Salisbury, foreign secretary in the British government. David Hill's letters home had frequently included comments concerning Mrs Hudson Taylor and her team, with the result that, unusually for a 'missionary wife', she was mentioned in his eventual biography, along with the fact that no other mission sent women to the region. A joint LMS and Bible Society meeting in London chaired by Lord Shaftesbury highlighted the work of the CIM in the famine above other groups, and within the citation 'the conduct of the heroic lady Mrs Taylor' was singled out for special mention. Messrs Richard, Turner and Hill were rewarded by the Chinese government with the offer of Mandarin rank – which they politely declined.

And eventually in Pingyang in southern Shansi a 6ft stone monument was erected in honour of those who came to China's rescue; the names inscribed were those of Hill, Richard and Turner – it would surely only have been the gender-based sense of propriety of the time that prevented one female name being added to the venerable list.

Meanwhile at home Hudson Taylor, still feeling the benefit of his Swiss holiday, started itinerating again. Keeping his finger on the Mission pulse, he wrote to Mr Broomhall from city after city across the Midlands and the north of England. His letters beginning 'Dear Benj' – considerably less flowery than the usual endearments of the time – always included the inevitable updates on how overstretched he was. His profile had increased to the point that he was beginning to receive invitations to speak at gatherings in European cities. It occurred to him that he could fulfil a short European itinerary on his way to China – and to his beloved Jennie. After the Christmas holidays with the family, therefore, and sad goodbyes to the children once again, he began his staged journey to China via Europe.

By the February (of 1879), Jennie decided she had done as much as she could in terms of her work in Taiyuen. Ongoing management could now be left in the hands of

Anna and Celia, who stayed long-term in the region, and on 11 February, Jennie started the long journey back to Tientsin; from here the steamer returned her to Shanghai, where she would eventually meet up with Hudson; she knew she could continue to be of influence there, where communications were so much better. Shansi was, after all, such an 'out-of-the-way region', she wrote home.

At this time also, Benjamin Broomhall, having relinquished his work with the Anti-Slavery Association, was now officially recognised as general secretary, responsible for day-to-day running of the CIM at home. William Soltau was still deputy, and Hudson's reliable long-term friend Theodore Howard became UK director, effectively replacing Hudson Taylor on the home front. These appointments contributed considerably to facilitating Hudson's departure, at about the same time as his wife was setting out to meet him.

On 25 February, Hudson was in Rotterdam, speaking at meetings. These were the first of many occasions on which he spoke via interpreter to Continental audiences. From Amsterdam he travelled to Paris, then to Cannes, to visit Mr Berger and his new bride, a much younger Swiss lady. As with the Taylors' own experience of second marriage, it was good she had known and loved the first Mrs Berger. From there he travelled to Marseilles, his usual port of embarkation for China.

By Naples he was feeling unwell again. Writing from here, for the first time he discussed a 'writing machine': the typewriter was beginning to make its appearance. In Port Said he mentioned he was treating his diarrhoea with 'chalk and opium'; a similar if more sophisticated combination was still in use a century later.

By 18 April he was still far from well – but the end was in sight and he would soon feel Jennie's loving arms and caring touch. She had been in Shanghai for a month already, watching impatiently 'on tiptoe of expectation', as day after day each 'French mail' disgorged its passengers onto the quay.

16

The Sanatorium of China (1879–81)

Jennie and Hudson were reunited in Shanghai on 23 April 1879. Their separation this time had been for 'only' eleven months, but it still represented painful if God-honouring sacrifice as far as they were concerned. For Jennie, there was the continuing separation from her children, with milestones missed forever, and made even more acute by the knowledge Hudson had so recently been with them. He brought photos back with him – but these were no substitute, and anyway Jennie felt some were 'not a good group'. She asked her mother to take Amy and Ernie to get better ones done. She also explained to her mother she had actually come to the conclusion that sacrifices of separation made by parents (meaning more herself than her mother) would somehow in turn be used by God to bring blessing to their children.

Hudson rallied somewhat on arrival in Shanghai – the joy of being with Jennie always worked wonders – but he was soon unwell again, and barely coping with the quantity of mail awaiting him. Someone suggested that in order to escape the suffocating heat of summer, they would do well to steam straight up the coast to Chefoo, 'the sanatorium of China'.

They docked in the port of Yantai; Jennie had called here briefly on her way up to Tientsin the previous year; for Hudson it was all unknown territory, territory nevertheless which was destined to become of vital importance to the life and work of the CIM. Chefoo was just a small fishing village at the opposite end of the bay, but it had somehow given its name to the whole area.

Chefoo's climate was revitalising, cold in winter, warm and balmy in summer: it had developed a reputation for being something of a resort, enjoyed by foreigners and wealthy Chinese alike. The Taylors were invited to share the home of some friends there for as long as they needed it. At first it seemed whenever Hudson ventured inland or back to the South, whether from overwork or change in climate he was ill again, and had to return to Chefoo to recover. Jennie despaired of ever succeeding in persuading him to moderate his workload, and it took until the end of the year (1879) before he was back to full strength. She was also surprised at how quickly she was missing him again whenever he was away, especially when news came that he was ill in the South. 'How I should like to be of more use in the world!' was her ironic exclamation in a letter sent home at that time.

But when he was in Chefoo it was like a holiday, with picnics on the beach and boat trips out to the island. She enjoyed having saltwater baths, and in writing to her parents returned to another of her themes, of how wonderful missionary life could be: 'I hope we shall not get spoiled here'.

During his slow recovery in Chefoo, Hudson spent time sitting and looking out across the calm, sheltered waters of the bay; as he inhaled the sweet sea air, plans began to formulate in his ever-active mind. What the Mission really needed here was a convalescent home; the thought soon developed into the possibilities of a hospital. Then what about a school for the children of missionaries – to enable parents and offspring to at least remain on the same side of the world as each other?

Almost as soon as his ideas had been shared with others, the CIM was offered some land to purchase, near the seashore and at a good price. Hudson Taylor drew up his own plans for a large house, local labour was employed and timber was used from a recent nearby shipwreck – including whole doors and cupboards. Meanwhile Mr and Mrs Judd had arrived. Mrs Judd, friend and co-worker to Jennie back in Hangchow, was very ill and in need of the Chefoo air. This first building, completed in record time, became their home for a while.

Now there would be no let-up as far as Hudson Taylor's plans were concerned, although subsequent buildings were constructed more slowly and purposefully. Gradually a sanatorium appeared, then a dispensary and a chapel, then finally (for the time being), a school.

Meanwhile, a Mr Elliston had had to withdraw from his inland missionary work, needing recovery time in Chefoo. Hudson suggested while he regained his health he could make use of his original teaching qualification, and take on the education of the Judds' three sons. Thus, Chefoo School began – with three pupils in a room in the Judds' new home. The China Inland Mission Protestant Collegiate School, as it was eventually and properly called ('collegiate' was considered to indicate 'boarding'), was officially founded in 1881, with Mr Elliston as its first headmaster. There would eventually be three schools, a girls', a boys' and a primary, with excellent premises and credentials, right through until the Second World War. In time they included fee-paying children from business and diplomatic families, delighted to find a microcosm of English 'public school' education on the shores of China's Yellow Sea.

Throughout these exciting developments, Jennie was relieved to be back at her husband's side. Whether caring for him in sickness, or travelling and ministering to others alongside him when he was strong again, she was doing what she most wanted to do. But she found her mind was often elsewhere. Try as she might, she could not erase from her memory the harrowing images from her recent experience. Hudson had shared her challenges through months of correspondence – but he had not been there. He had not witnessed first-hand those awful sights and sounds. The deathly faces of so many who had arrived for help were now parading unbidden across her mind.

It was a relief to her, a healing balm, to turn her thoughts into prayers for those still at work in Taiyuen. But at times she caught herself worrying as she thought of the orphans and other victims to whom she had had to say goodbye. She knew some would not have survived.

She had been so immersed, in a sense so happy in the work, yet she knew it was right to leave when she did. Why was it now such a struggle?

While snatches of scenes still haunted her, she had forgotten much of what she had actually achieved; at the time she kept no record, nor did she have time to write many letters, but afterwards she did write a booklet-length account for their children of why she had felt prompted to go. She dwelt on the initial decision, describing at length her anxieties about doing the right thing. She enlarged on her theory that they would be blessed because of their parents' sacrifices. This theme was positively picked up, particularly by Hudson's daughter Maria, who responded by expressing her understanding that the 'sacrifice' was actually to be shouldered by them also, thereby releasing a greater sense of God's love in their own lives.

She shared with them too how much her illness in Nanking had rocked her confidence: she had worried about being a burden during the long and difficult journey to Taiyuen. It was all a path she would not have chosen, she explained, but with the confidence of a reward for them all as a family, as well as fulfilling God's greater purposes. Saying she 'did not keep any account' while she was there, instead she painted a picture of how much she missed them now! She could imagine them here, she said, running along the seashore, and having picnics together on the sand.

She included the details of the nightmarish journey she and their father had recently shared in order to reach Chefoo, how she had been responsible for spoon-feeding him when he was so ill, milk being all he could manage, while fog was bringing the ship to a virtual standstill: 'Would Papa live to the end of the journey?' These were all lessons she had learned in faith and trust, she said – ones that they would surely need to learn also. The children were certainly leading extraordinary lives. This altogether heady emotional mix would have to be skilfully and positively managed within the loving Broomhall household: laughter, fun, and much grace would probably be as important as lessons in faith and trust.

Gradually Jennie's unhelpful memories receded, replaced by other memories which were prized: she had seen ancient and mysterious cave dwellings in the vast moonscape of the *loess* plateau, she had enjoyed autumn's vibrant maple colours alongside the track across the mountains to Taiyuen, and she had watched majestic camel caravans arriving from the Silk Road, with its links to colder and more distant lands. And she had got on so well with Mr Richard and others leading the relief. She was disappointed when she realised Timothy Richard didn't always see eye-to-eye with her husband's more long-term policy and approach to mission.

Hudson Taylor's attitude to his wife's singular and truly amazing accomplishment was one of immense pride; but he also knew it represented a daring departure from normal practice, as far as female missionaries were concerned. He felt it was an experiment which had succeeded, but he also knew not everyone saw it that way, so for a while he did not radically alter long-term plans. In time, however, single CIM women were indeed sent inland, penetrating further than even their role-model Mrs Taylor had gone, and fulfilling that vital task of reaching women in their homes and sheltered lives, in a way that men could never do.

It underlined the oft-discussed theory in missionary circles, that in fact women, who are far less of a threat, are therefore safer than their male colleagues in otherwise the most dangerous of unreached places.

By the December of that year (1879) the Taylors were back in Shanghai. On Christmas Day, disclosing a restlessness borne of being away from family, Jennie wrote to her parents: 'The dear children are all enjoying their Christmas I expect. What a miss it is not to have them around us!' and: 'It is a very real cross being parted from the dear children.' Perhaps it was a greater cross when she was not preoccupied and busy. At this point she did not even have anywhere to call home.

It was a constant yet ever-changing dilemma. It was known that 19-year-old Herbert was thinking seriously of a return to China. Could he perhaps bring Ernest and Amy with him to enable Jennie to stay longer by her husband's side? Perhaps he could help look after them when he arrived!

Meanwhile, of course, there were always presents from the Fauldings – not just at Christmastime, but throughout the year. Jennie had asked them for a special leather fold-up case for photos. As well as the portrait she had already requested of Ernie and Amy, she asked if she could have good ones of her parents themselves, as well as ones of William's and Alfred's 'groups', and one of Nellie's growing family; she would then have a 'complete set in portable form'. In the June she asked her parents for an update of all the children's photos. It pained both Hudson and Jennie if they dwelt on how much the children, particularly Jennie's two, would be changing.

One particular gift from home was treasured, and given frequent mention: it was a copy of *Kept for the Master's Use*, the newly published book by Frances Ridley Havergal, based on her currently popular hymn, 'Take my Life'.

Later her mother forwarded the *Life* of the famous hymn-writer and author; this had a profound effect on Jennie, and she was sure it would do 'immense good' for others also. Indeed, two female colleagues wrote pieces in *China's Millions* bearing testimony to the blessing of encountering Miss Havergal's writings through Mrs Taylor.

In the New Year, Hudson set off on his travels again. Always anxious to give his personal support to the growing number of stations, and often fulfilling a troubleshooting role, he visited as many as he could throughout south-eastern China; he spent time particularly at Yangchow, where his family had once had such a narrow escape from fire and riot, and now destined to become one of the CIM's two language schools, and also Wuchang (part of Wuhan, the vast 'three-in-one' city). Here in the March (of 1880) Jennie reached him by steamer up the Yangtze, and for a while they travelled together again.

By June they were back in Shanghai. Hudson wrote to Benjamin Broomhall that Jennie would be unable to accompany him for a while, as she was nursing a sick member of the Mission, a wife who was considered to be in a dangerous state – although she eventually recovered to live into her nineties. In the August, Hudson wrote that they had had to be apart for two months: but by the October they were together again in Chefoo.

Throughout this time, Jennie kept up with news from Shansi. The work in Taiyuen was going well, with both Anna Crickmay and Celia Horne settled and content. They reported positively on the continuing workshop and schools programmes among the children and women, with ongoing help from Mrs Richard. But even with the promise of a good harvest, practical relief was still desperately needed – the news of which, of course, had to be relayed home. In the February of the New Year (1881), not altogether surprisingly one of the two ladies, Miss Crickmay, married Mr Turner.

The pattern of Hudson's travels continued; he would so much have loved to have thrown himself once again into the pioneering activities of the growing number, males and now females, of new CIM recruits. But Chefoo was a blessing, currently something of an administrative centre for the Mission, and a retreat for the often-exhausted Hudson Taylor, where he could recover until the next trip. It was now Hudson's underlying state of health more than anything else which was preventing Jennie from making plans to return home to her children, which she was now longing to do.

Back in London, Mrs Taylor senior was paying a summer visit to Pyrland Road. With seventeen grandchildren there to be enjoyed, and her other daughter, Louisa, and family not living far away, there was plenty to keep her busy. But suddenly on 2 July 1881, while sitting quietly, Hudson's mother was taken from them. Amelia was relieved that at least her mother had been surrounded by family. Mr Taylor senior, not a healthy man himself, naturally came to stay for a while.

Hudson and Jennie heard quickly by telegram – but there was nothing they could do. This was just one of the many sacrifices of overseas service at that time. They certainly could not rush home to be present at the funeral. The burial took place in Abney Park Cemetery, one of London's new 'mega' cemeteries, and one specifically with provision for nonconformists.

It was Jennie's mother whom they knew to be deteriorating. Twice during the preceding year, indigestion had been mentioned, but the emphasis at first was positive, with expressions of hope on both sides of the globe that she would soon be better. In the December, Jennie had written to her mother that she was 'longing inexpressibly to come home again'; but there was no particular thought that she would not see her again, hoping the 'indigestion is a thing of the past'.

Hudson's ongoing quandary, of whether to respond to the needs at home or in China, was now extended to Jennie. He acknowledged she was needed at home – but how much he needed her by his side! Still, he was in the position to make proactive decisions. All Jennie could do was reassure her parents that she was trusting God for the right time ('and perhaps not very long') for her return.

On 18 May, a few weeks before the news of Hudson's mother, Jennie had written to her parents: 'I am longing and praying for the way to be opened for us to pay a visit home'. She was 'sorry not to hear a better account of improvement in your health'. But the tone was still upbeat, and included news that the Prince of Wales' sons were arriving in China on a visit; there were seven British gunboats standing by in the bay.

On 27 June, the tone changed. 'Who is nursing you?' she asked her mother, while also having to say that Hudson was too ill, and the summer 'too hot and trying' for him to be left. She was relieved to know her mother was not suffering – and that she could swallow again. She may now be coming home in October, she said. Every letter of Jennie's from now on somewhere included the words 'How I long . . . but . . .' within them.

On 25 July, not long after hearing of Mrs Taylor's demise, she wrote thanking her mother for exerting herself enough to write a letter dated 24 June. She was relieved that at least William and Alfred were around, and that Nellie and Charlie were still in London.

On 23 August she wrote again, thanking her mother for a letter dated 11 July – but ironically not only did Mrs Faulding's letter contain further details surrounding the death of Mrs Taylor, sadly Jennie's reply was dispatched after her mother had died! The telegram arrived on 24 August. Coming so quickly after news of Hudson's mother's death, it seemed more shocking as Jennie's mother was almost a decade younger than Hudson's. She had died on 13 August, and the burial had already taken place in Camden Cemetery, not far from their home in Barnet.

The mothers shared the same black-edged page in *China's Millions*. The double tribute was at once equitable, yet also in a way invidious, greater detail being provided concerning Mrs Taylor. Perhaps understandably she was honoured with a fuller appreciation on behalf of the Mission; the Fauldings, of course, had not made that radical dedication to China of the unborn Jane Elizabeth, as the Taylors had done of their anticipated child. But Jennie knew the true sacrifice of her mother giving two daughters to China. 'Nobody's letter takes the place of yours', she had once said.

This double bereavement was the prompt which released Jennie to travel home at last. She sailed from Yantai on 13 October 1881, accompanied by Celia Horne, who had been unwell since May. The new Mrs Turner was relieved as she had been concerned that her marriage would mean abandoning Miss Horne, her one-time colleague. For the Taylors, however, another separation seemed unavoidable.

While Jennie was on her way home, Hudson received an unbelievable third telegram: it brought news that his father had collapsed and died, also unexpectedly, at home in his garden. The news eventually caught up with Jennie *poste restante* in Port Said.

Fittingly in a way at the close of this year of loss for Hudson and Jennie, the black-edged tribute to Mr Taylor was the last entry on the very last page of the December 1881 edition of *China's Millions*.

But for Hudson, who had just waved goodbye to his wife, a rare treat was on the way, as he stood again on the dockside at Shanghai.

17

Who Will Look After My Boy? (1881–84)

Hudson's concerns for the field were now compounded by worries of finding the right teachers for Chefoo; he had not anticipated this would be a problem, and characteristically he felt responsible. Part of the solution was about to present itself, however. In the December (of 1881), at about the time his wife was reaching home, there was a compensatory blessing for Hudson: with gratitude and tears of joy he watched his eldest son, Herbert, step ashore on his first return to China. As his father before him, he had chosen to put his medical studies aside, in Herbert's case to join the teaching staff at Chefoo. They went first to see his mother's grave.

But now without Jennie, life did not get easier for Hudson. He was constantly torn: worrying about London, with the financial, administrative and recruiting needs, and almost overwhelmed in China, with his constant pastoral and organisational responsibilities for his scattered and growing team. Among the many excellent new recruits being sent out there were some entirely unsuited – even one or two troublemakers. Should he be on the field to pick up the pieces, or at home to overhaul the process?

The quandary continued. With Jennie gone, he now yearned more than ever for the shores of England, but one crisis after another weighed in favour of his remaining in China. The latest challenge to preoccupy him was that of ancestor worship.

As far as the Chinese were concerned, ancestor worship was non-negotiable: it took precedence over whether or not they practised Taoism, Buddhism or Confucianism. The problem for some missionaries was that there appeared to be degrees of commitment to the ancient practice: at one end of the spectrum, it seemed to be little more than maintaining respectful memory; at the other, it descended into a communing with ancestral spirits. Some missionaries such as Timothy Richard, in an honest attempt to enable the Chinese more easily to accept Christianity, felt the innocuous end could do no harm. Hudson was troubled that some CIM missionaries were becoming influenced by these and other possibly liberal views.

Jennie, meanwhile, having arrived home on 1 December, was delighted to be back with the children; she was also almost immediately thrust into the centre of the work – as with Emily, so many years before, she was now the Council's most obvious link with what was happening on the ground in China, and with their leader. This meant her letters to Hudson inevitably became more business-like; it appeared to Hudson she was not picking up on his heart-cry for something more intimate. He was also deeply discouraged that remittances were not being sent from the committee when they should; he wrote that now there was even less excuse, with the telegraphic transfer (of money) being available. Communication with London was confused, and they were still having issues among themselves! 'With a director and a responsible Sec at home . . . you should be independent of me for home matters', he had written to Benjamin Broomhall.

He had a way of letting people know in his correspondence when he was almost beside himself with worry, having responsibility for so much and so many; at the same time, he would state he was not concerned, his trust being steadfastly in God. This made it difficult for recipients, above all for Jennie, who needed to know just how to offer emotional support. In March, after one particularly exhausting journey, he wrote: 'I feel as if my journeying days were almost over'; he contemplated staying just for another year or so, then returning home for good. With practised and prayerful wisdom, Jennie learned exactly how to respond to such propositions.

Additionally, his multiple preoccupations caused the inevitable return of his stress-related dysentery, weakening him just when he felt alone and in need of strength. He would share these and other health problems also, then after a short period of recuperation wonder why Jennie's letters, inevitably caught in the time lag, were expressing such concern. He never developed his wife's knack of waiting until the crisis was over before sharing it.

At home, when not spending time with the family or dealing with administrative concerns alongside the Council, Jennie turned to the piles of correspondence awaiting her on the elegant 'secretaire' in the corner of her room. In the

May she addressed Lord Radstock, asking him to pass on thanks to his Russian Christian friends for their gift.

Then quite by chance she found a new area of vital activity.

She had picked up a copy of *The Christian Traveller's Handbook* – and made an exciting discovery: an advertisement for Mrs Grimké's Scripture cards.

Emma Grimké and her American husband, Theodore, were busy in evangelistic and philanthropic work in the slums of Manchester. Emma had noticed how dreary the homes of the poor were: brightly coloured cards with a picture and a Bible text might be just the thing to make all the difference. She designed a selection and had them printed, and soon these were decorating the damp walls in many dwellings, much to the pride and delight of the inhabitants, whilst also providing opportunities to share the message of the text, even to those who could not read. They proved to be popular with inner-city missions across Britain, and soon they were taken up by Continental missions also, being translated eventually into a remarkable eight European languages. In time, Mrs Grimké's contacts and influence were even more widespread; she was contacted by workers in Arab then Indian missions: her cards were eventually translated into an amazing fifty languages! They were specifically for distribution by missionaries and Christian travellers, and were particularly popular with women. Jennie wasted no time in ordering as many as she could in Chinese, and was soon sending them out to her colleagues on the field. They were soon contacting her asking for more. It seemed to matter not at all that the recipients were often illiterate, or that the bucolic scenes on the cards were so English. They were brightly coloured and received eagerly, and gave ample opportunity for an explanation of the message.

The cards were 'like a door', one missionary reported in *China's Millions*.

Jennie was also a main speaker at one of the farewell services taking place for the latest wave of departing missionaries. She addressed a packed congregation in the cavernous Westbourne Grove Baptist Chapel. Now a seasoned speaker, she was able to paint vivid scenes of Chinese life which would at once fascinate yet also challenge her audience. She also mentioned something new in their hearing: she talked about the Seventy. This was a concept which Hudson had discussed with her in his letters while she was travelling home.

He had arrived at this figure after prayer and discussion with colleagues while in Wuchang. Employing his usual 'missionary maths', he had worked out that fifty or sixty new recruits, both men and women, could usefully be situated throughout China's provinces as soon as possible. It was the story of Jesus sending out seventy workers which prompted him to start praying specifically for that number.

Later in the year, as the summer heat returned, Hudson once again travelled to Chefoo. As well as giving time to plan both for a medical college and for outlying opium refuges across China, he drafted an appeal to the home churches, with the concept of the Seventy – to be sent out 'within three years' – in mind. In no way did he paint a rosy picture of how easy it would be: he warned of hardships and illness for even the most intrepid. This undoubtedly had a salutary effect on response to start with, and in spite of valiant efforts at publicity on the part of the London Council, there were few enquiries or offers of financial support for the rest of that year.

In the January of 1883 the balance in favour of Hudson being at home began to tip at last. To Jennie's eventual relief, he wrote a letter on the 23rd saying he was making definite arrangements for a return, and was letting his hair grow out in readiness. His plan was to travel first to Chefoo to see Herbert, then as usual to pick up the French packet in Hong Kong. From this time on, from whichever side of the globe he was setting off, he was going to have to say goodbye to at least one of his children.

On 6 February, Hudson set sail from Chefoo. In the coming weeks, during his voyage home, answers to prayers for the Seventy began to be seen at last. A massive gift of £3,000 arrived from one donor. The tide was starting to turn, due in no small part to Mr Broomhall's skills at public relations; China's 'needs and claims' were coming to the forefront of church awareness, for some for the first time.

When Hudson reached Marseilles, as was now his normal practice he dispatched most of his luggage to be taken the rest of the way by ship, while he travelled overland from this point. He spent a few days with Mr Berger and his new wife in Cannes then, as he had business to see to in Paris, arranged to have Jennie meet him there. He had written almost daily to her, barely able to suppress his anticipation at seeing her again. His letters were passionate – some members of the next generation even went as far as redacting one or two sentences!

Springtime in Paris, when they had been apart for so long, was not going to disappoint. When on Good Friday his train eventually pulled in at *Gare de Lyon*, Jennie was there at the barrier to meet him. They had barely the Easter weekend alone in each other's company, and some of that was catching up on business, but now they were together at last, time no longer seemed to matter.

By the time they reached London, Hudson had picked up on all the encouraging news. Some friends of the Mission had struggled at first with the idea of expansion when funds were low, but now positive excitement was spreading. Applications to join the Seventy were multiplying; initially it came as a shock for him to learn that his own 16-year-old Maria, plus the two eldest Broomhall 'children', wished to be counted in that number. Finances were coming in also: Mr Berger had followed up on Hudson's visit with a £500 donation, and with expressions of ongoing and unswerving support, as ever, for his dear friend.

As a result of Benjamin Broomhall's hard work at publicity, invitations for Hudson to speak were pouring in from across the kingdom. It seemed that at last the pioneering work of the CIM had caught the imagination of the churches: in Christian circles Hudson Taylor was beginning to be a household name. In the July he was in Keswick for the now well-established convention. From there he travelled to Belfast.

The Mission still had supporters in high places. Hudson Taylor's upper-class and titled friends were still among his greatest encouragers, and he became quite used to staying in grand country houses where large groups had been assembled to hear him. After a tour of church gatherings in Belfast, he travelled straight to the wilds of Northumberland to stay with the Tankervilles in Chillingham Castle.

The atmosphere was a revitalising blessing: 'Lady Tankerville has given me the run of the Castle', he wrote excitedly to Jennie, and 'today is the first day of grouse-shooting' – but alas, it was raining.

All this involved more separation again; but times and distances were shorter now, and often too Jennie was free to accompany her husband. She had been with him in Keswick, and now after his stay in Northumberland, Hudson arranged to meet her roughly halfway home in Bakewell, Derbyshire; they shared a deep-rooted appreciation of beautiful countryside, so as well as the uplift of encouraging meetings, they were reinvigorated by the rugged moorland scenery of the Dales.

Everywhere Hudson went, his speaking and preaching were as warmly received as ever; his style remained quiet and unassuming, but if anything what he said seemed now even more anointed and powerful in its effect. Also, in the August he drafted his thoughts, putting them in a circular letter, on the proposition of dividing the whole of the Chinese 'field' into districts, with a council and a superintendent for each district. This was eventually agreed by the London Council, and proved so helpful in principle that with adaptations it remained in place for more than a hundred years.

The sense of momentum continued on into 1884. It was clear prayers for the Seventy had been abundantly answered, and in fact it was eighty-four new recruits in all who had left for China, not in three years, but by the end of that year.

In the September, the Taylors' close friends Lord and Lady Radstock were away for a month; they handed over their beautiful home in Richmond, Surrey to Hudson and Jennie, Ernest, Amy and Millie, to use at their leisure; it was welcome at an otherwise emotional time. On 21 September the farewell service took place in the Mildmay Conference Hall for twenty-eight young people, all single, and Maria Taylor, as well as Gertrude and Hudson Broomhall, were among them. For passage-booking reasons, including segregation of the sexes some, including young Maria, had already sailed. This probably made it easier for the main speaker, who happened to be her father! Maria would be joining her brother in Chefoo. Gertrude and Hudson departed with six others in the following few days. As it happened, albeit unknown at the time, Herbert Taylor's future wife was 'farewelled' at the same meeting. As for the Mission's funds, there was never going to be a surfeit, but income was better now than it had been for a long time.

And the spiritual impetus, and its effect on people's lives, continued to grow.

At the same time as all the other encouragements of 1884, in terms of enquiries and recruitment a new front appeared to be opening up: interest had been growing amongst Britain's university students, with particular activity centring in Cambridge. The Cambridge Seven, as they were eventually and famously known, were representative of this new groundswell. All privately educated in the UK's most prestigious schools, five of them had then graduated from Cambridge, and two were from a military background; all keen and successful sportsmen, they were also very wealthy. These were all virtues highly esteemed in the public's eyes. But as the cream of privileged British society, they were thought by many, in pursuing an interest

Who Will Look After My Boy? (1881–84)

in going as missionaries to China, to be throwing their lives away. But each one of the Cambridge Seven had had a radical conversion experience, mainly through hearing Hudson Taylor's friend, the American evangelist Mr Moody, and all had been deeply touched by the message of God's love for the lost of China. They had already launched out from their opulent backgrounds and had begun to prove their trust in God in work among the destitute of England's cities.

For the parents, however, particularly the mothers, this was all terribly hard. Four of the six mothers (two of the 'Seven' being brothers) were particularly upset, and were in correspondence with Jennie. They were hardly expecting Jennie to change their sons' minds, but in the words of one mother she (Jennie) would be sympathetic as she 'knows something of separation from family'. Some requested a few minutes of Jennie's time; others put their requests in writing. Things had moved too quickly as far as they were all concerned.

Lady Beauchamp felt that her son should sail out with Hudson Taylor to 'drink into [his] views'. Mrs Studd had travelled to London hoping to see Jennie: she wrote from her fashionable Hyde Park address. She was confused by several issues, not least that the CIM had returned a cheque. Her son had gladly turned his back on wealth, giving away his earthly goods in happy identity with CIM's financial stance, and Hudson Taylor's apparent vow of poverty. But surely, she wrote, with his background he would be expected to contribute more than his fair share of funds. There again, for his own comfort and needs for the journey, he must surely be allowed to provide for himself. She was sorry that his passage to China would be second class. After all, if he were in first class he could relate downwards – but it wouldn't work the other way round. And at first Mrs Cassels couldn't get past the question of why her ordained son could not work at home 'for the same Master', rather than go to China.

Towards the end of 1884, the Cambridge Seven were taking part in a succession of highly successful speaking tours. Mrs Studd wrote: 'I am very distressed at my son's erratic movements and going off to Scotland without any clothes . . . except those he had on.' In this, Mrs Studd collaborated with Mrs Smith, as their sons were travelling together. As a foretaste of their life in China they saw no problem at all in surviving a week in Scotland with only one shirt each. 'He fancies he needs nothing', was Mrs Smith's comment, from her address in Berkeley Square. Both mothers felt their respective sons were too similar to each other: '[They] are too much of the same impulsive nature and one excites the other', wrote Mrs Studd. She wished for her son to be placed alongside 'an older and more consistent-minded Christian to do quiet and steady work'.

There was more than a hint of 'Who will look after my boy?' in the struggling letters. The considerable handicap for boys whose cosseted experience had been the upper-class path of exclusive schooling followed by university, under normal circumstances would go unnoticed, but a future life requiring self-reliance found them, certainly as far as their mothers were concerned, with a near-total inability to look after themselves. Hudson Taylor had seen to all his personal and practical needs during his own student years; helping these women over this difficult hurdle was a new

Who Will Look After My Boy? (1881–84)

and unexpected challenge for Jennie, and it came to occupy much of her time in coming months.

Hudson Taylor felt he should return to China to work with this unusual band of men – and planned to get there ahead of them. Once again it would have to be without Jennie. This would be his sixth journey to China. Jennie at this stage had completed a mere three.

By any reckoning, as Victorian travellers, they were now in the elite category!

18

Even Queen Victoria Received Her Copy (1885–89)

Hudson Taylor left for China on 20 January 1885. The Taylors were once again looking at an agony of parting, with months of separation ahead.

The children too had to say goodbye to their father, so Jennie decided to stay with them rather than travel to Dover to wave him off. She therefore had many hours to endure of knowing he was still on British soil, but out of reach. Amelia, ever a strong emotional support, came next door to put her arms round her sister-in-law, and spend a while with her.

Now there were just days left before the departure of the Cambridge Seven – but days filled with amazing events. The Seven were addressing huge crowds in Oxford, Cambridge and London; momentum was growing, especially among many curious students, drawn by the call to a radical lifestyle, but more importantly to their own need for God. The gatherings were spoken well of in high places also: Revd Handley Moule, himself a Cambridge man and soon to be

Even Queen Victoria Received Her Copy (1885–89) 193

Bishop of Durham, declared the meetings to be the most remarkable he had experienced. This was encouragement indeed and, as it happened, of huge relevance to Jennie. It was the familiarity of that surname! It set off in her mind an unfortunate echo from many years ago; few others would know the significance.

Most of the *Lammermuir* party, if they had not already died, were active in China. Jennie alone was brought up with a start as she remembered those early months in Hangchow when Moule's two older brothers, themselves both clerics and missionaries to China, were deeply critical of Hudson Taylor and the ways of the CIM. The hurt of the whole episode briefly threatened to swamp her again, but her forgiving spirit enabled her to delight in this new endorsement, recognising it more than made up for the trauma of two decades previously.

The 'Farewell' meetings finished with the biggest audience of all, of more than five thousand, in London's vast Exeter Hall just off the Strand. This was on 4 February, the day of the Cambridge Seven's planned departure. But clamour for this one final meeting had been such that Jennie and Benjamin agreed the P&O should be contacted, in order to arrange for the Seven to leave a day later and travel overland, catching up with their ship in Brindisi, Italy. So the fact they were departing the very next day seemed to add an urgent charge to the atmosphere in the Exeter Hall. 'What shall I say?' Benjamin Broomhall exclaimed in a letter to Hudson: 'Such a meeting!'

Even the Seven's longsuffering mothers were bowing to the inevitable: all spoke warmly of the meetings, much to Jennie's relief, as being times of great blessing. Mrs Cassels was now asking somewhat tardily which Chinese Bible she should buy for her son. Mrs Studd, however, was worrying about how to get money to her son when once he arrived in China. With Hudson out of reach, even more responsibility for last-minute preparation descended onto Jennie: there were still so few in London with first-hand experience of China.

When once the party had finally left, Jennie picked up on some speaking engagements. She had two bookings on the Isle of Wight in March. Most of the Cambridge Seven mothers decided to have a regular 'tea-meeting' on Wednesdays at Lady Beauchamp's. They had all been moved by what they had witnessed, and wished to commit to ongoing regular prayer. Jennie attended when she could: they needed her guidance in this new endeavour.

Hudson arrived in Shanghai on 3 March. No sooner had he arrived than he had to take receipt of a parcel from Mrs Studd. Hudson had evidently suggested that, in order to help alleviate her concerns about her son, and to bypass his ascetic tendency, Mrs Studd could send a few possessions on ahead without his knowing. This had disastrous results. Would he really be pleased to see a table laid waiting for him, complete with knives, forks and napkins? As frequently happened, Jennie's role the other side of the globe was to pick up the pieces. This was difficult, as she endeavoured to bring encouragement to the mothers' Wednesday meetings.

On 18 March, the Cambridge Seven arrived in Shanghai – and at first they didn't recognise the Chinaman waving to them from the dockside. It was Hudson Taylor, there to welcome them.

It wasn't long before Hudson was sending letters of tender longing to Jennie again, sometimes employing Romanised Ningpo or Hangchow, presumably to convey his feelings. She still featured in his dreams, and these, plus the searing pain of waking up, were all shared in his letters, mixed in with prosaic business details as they occurred to him.

Meanwhile, she was kept busy assisting Benjamin with selecting and editing correspondence suitable for the monthly *China's Millions* (although it went out in Hudson Taylor's name). And the annual compilation, beautifully bound and embossed, was still being produced: even Queen Victoria received her copy. Eventually, in a similar large presentation format, Benjamin Broomhall compiled and edited the story of the Cambridge Seven, entitled *A Missionary Band.* Ten thousand copies were sold within the first few months.

Then in the April came the first intimation, from China, of a romance in the Taylor family. Hudson was already impressed with J.J. (Joe) Coulthard; he had known him since they travelled out together in 1879. They had on occasion itinerated together, and got on well, so the surprise of his declaration of love for Maria was entirely acceptable. It now fell to Jennie to visit, and become acquainted with, his parents in London. It was agreed they would wait a while to marry, as Maria was still only 18, but they soon became officially engaged. Hudson felt the relationship did wonders for his daughter, transforming her into womanhood. Then another surprise: in the August, his son Herbert became engaged to Jeanie Gray. For the time being, Maria remained working at Chefoo. The school was expanding, with separate buildings now for boys and girls.

Hudson characteristically continued to carry a sense of personal responsibility for staffing.

In June, Hudson commented in a letter to Jennie that two of the Cambridge Seven were 'getting it wrong already'; then in a following letter he reported that two others were 'over-fasting'. This placed yet another challenge firmly in Jennie's lap, to be handled diplomatically at the Wednesday meeting. On a more positive note, they were pleased their sons were making good use of the 'Mrs Grimké' visiting cards which they had sent out. Later that year Mrs Polhill-Turner, mother of the two brothers, joined the weekly meetings. And so they continued to meet, being now totally supportive of all that was going on with their sons in China.

And the Seven themselves? In the long-term, demonstrating key leadership and pioneering abilities, they all matured, in their differing ways, into highly effective and faithful missionaries.

It was also in the June that some land came up for sale in Wusong Road, Shanghai. A large gift had been given for the purchase of a building suitable for a China HQ, so the purchase of the land went ahead. The building was completed by 1890, and was to serve the purposes of the CIM well for forty years. At this time the two language training centres, Anking for the men and Yangchow for the women, were established. They were both, as it happened, places of past riot and persecution – Jennie shuddered to recall what she had known of the sufferings of some of the *Lammermuir* team in Yangchow – but they would henceforth be places of much blessing.

Much to Jennie's relief, Hudson appointed John Stevenson as his deputy in China from this time; even Hudson had to agree the burden of responsibility was now undeniably too great for just one man. Mr Stevenson was one of the very few CIM workers who had arrived before the *Lammermuir*, and was therefore of long-term proven faithfulness. Through his new China Council, Hudson instructed all the stations that Mr Stevenson would visit and support where he himself was unable to. It was Jennie's dearest wish that the arrangement would work – which it did, beyond Hudson's directorship, well into the next century.

There was always a need within Hudson and Jennie's correspondence for discussion and decision-making relating to the children. Howard was still studying medicine at the London Hospital, and was suggesting it would help him considerably, and save money, if he could stay and have his dinner at the hospital every day. What did his father think? Money was a consideration even with their mother's endowment; Charles had two more years at school; but was boarding really an option, even with reduced rates for ministers' sons, while Howard's education was not completed? On the other hand, a year or so away from home could be a good thing, as had been proved with Howard. By November 1887 Charlie was writing from the Leys School, a Methodist foundation in Cambridgeshire, where he described himself as a 'Wesleyan undergrad'.

In spite of now having a deputy, Hudson continued to work at full stretch. 'I do not know how to get more work out of myself than I do' was his latest way of describing a very familiar state of affairs. His own surprising response to this self-imposed challenge came in the same letter: 'I am learning Pitman's shorthand, and so is Herbert. Will you learn it too?' Then came the suggestions as to what Jennie would need in order to join in this transcontinental family activity: first a manual, then the *Phonetic Journal* at a penny a week, to receive regular exercises. The irony was apparently missed that it was a skill that would tend to generate yet more work. The 'Frenetic Journal' might have been more apt.

Towards the end of 1886, Hudson was feeling it was time to return home. He had at last visited Shansi, a province Jennie knew well. He sent her a letter from the capital, Taiyuen, including a good report of Mr and Mrs Turner (née Anna Crickmay, one of Jennie's companions during the famine) still well settled there. Sadly, however, Hudson's health let him down once more; his dysentery returned, preventing him from getting out and about and seeing something of the city which had been his wife's home for almost a year. Although probably a stress-related inflammatory bowel problem, he put his symptoms down to the 'churning motion of the litter' on the long journey overland from Tientsin. As often, Jennie was apprised of the details of just how bad the current attack was!

In spite of his incapacity, Hudson Taylor spoke with powerful effect at conferences in Taiyuen, and also in Pingyang (the city of southern Shansi where the stone monument had been erected to the heroes of the famine). Many present, from other missions also, reported glorious times of great blessing.

What was it about Shansi? All China's greatest problems – famines, floods, the scourge of opium, the current ravages of smallpox – together with perhaps her greatest spiritual blessings – all were writ large in Shansi. This great northern province was a microcosm of the very worst and yet the very best of missionary experience. And within the next decade or so there was much more to come. Jennie knew something of Shansi's extremes; she had shared in its sorrows and joys, and was glad she could identify easily with her husband's progress.

The final event of significance before Hudson's departure was the convening, in Anking, of the first China Council – when he and John Stevenson met with the newly appointed directors of the work in the provinces, fine-tuning and establishing the *Principles and Practice*, which each new candidate must sign, together with the *Book of Arrangements*, ground rules as it were for a now large, widespread, and potentially unwieldy organisation.

Hudson planned to set off on his homeward journey in the New Year. In the December, as he prepared to leave, he commented to Jennie on the passing of yet another of their wedding anniversaries (28 November). 'One more wedding day was passed apart! How many of them have been so spent?' (The answer was six out of a possible fifteen at this point.) But that November had brought a cause to celebrate, as Herbert, 25, married his sweetheart, Jeanie, who was 23; she had travelled out at the same time as Maria. Jennie shared Hudson's delight at the happy news.

Maria for the time being continued to live with Herbert and his new wife; and often Hudson was under their roof. He found this was an enormous blessing: 'I believe they both know me better than ever before and are more sonly and daughterly in their feelings than ever before.'

And again: 'God has made me so rich in the love of my dear children.' God was certainly honouring all the years of absentee parenting and extreme self-sacrifice on Hudson's part. What Herbert and Maria must have missed in stability – and a mother's love – was now partly being compensated for by their father's warm attentiveness and demonstrative nature, so unusual in Victorian men.

Hudson set sail on 6 January 1887. When the telegram arrived giving Jennie the instructions as to where to meet him in Paris, she felt almost weak with excitement: 'I shall try to get the March CM [*China's Millions*] ready early so as to be free to enjoy you.'

Their train from Dover took them into the heart of the City of London, thanks to the newly built Blackfriars Bridge and St Paul's Station (later renamed Blackfriars Station). Arriving home, it didn't take Hudson long to realise it was the year of Queen Victoria's Golden Jubilee. Her Silver had not been celebrated due to the death of Prince Albert, and she was now just beginning to reappear after what had been effectively twenty-five years of mourning. The public, and after due persuasion the Queen also, were allowing themselves to begin to be excited: decorations were appearing, and plans were mounting for tremendous celebrations. Buffalo Bill and his Wild West Show were being shipped across the Atlantic for a grand mega-performance in May, and celebrations would climax with a glorious thanksgiving service in Westminster Abbey in June. But for the China Inland Mission, 1887 would be the year of the Hundred.

Hudson had already begun discussing plans for this new initiative with Jennie. As it happened, Mr Stevenson had also written excitedly to her about it. He fully expected that God would rebuke them and send more.

As soon as Hudson was home, he started to travel, and more often than not he was accompanied by Jennie. The now teenage and increasingly helpful Millie occasionally went along also. Ernie and Amy were old enough to cope without their mother for short periods, in the familiarity of the extended Pyrland Road family. Although to a certain extent still torn, by her husband's side was where Jennie felt she most belonged. And frequently she would have speaking engagements of her own: when they were in Glasgow, she was invited to address the YWCA.

Being with Hudson exacerbated Jennie's concerns. She noted in Edinburgh that it was 'one unbroken succession of meetings, interviews, correspondence, crowding one upon another . . . all he could do with all my help.' Neither was he getting the time with the children which he would have liked. But they were both full of praise to God for the heart-warming responses, personal and financial, as a result of the meetings.

Jennie was only too aware that not all was sweetness between the London Council and her husband when in China. The combined challenges of distance and personalities were at times insuperable. It was a relief to her, naturally protective of Hudson, to see them once more in the same room, praying and talking together. While there was agreement in principle over plans to accept and send out the Hundred, it was also acknowledged it would put enormous pressure on the CIM's current housing stock, to say nothing of the Broomhall family themselves. All the CIM homes in Pyrland Road, whether rented or owned, were now full to overflowing; as well as basic family accommodation there was a constant stream of candidates and other visitors, and a growing need for office space. (The Mission also had possession of five houses further along the road, originally purchased by Mr Taylor senior when he retired from the Barnsley Permanent Building Society, as income for Amelia – but these were not currently occupied by the CIM.)

Round the corner Newington Green, still with its duck pond, retained something of the village about it. It was fast developing the atmosphere and prestige of the leafy suburb, however, now with some handsome properties immediately surrounding the green – and remarkably, one of those properties, with land attached, came up for sale. In the July (of 1887) a contract was signed to purchase Inglesby House, as it was called. From the early eighteenth century, Newington Green had been an area favoured by Dissenters; a Unitarian chapel dating from that time still overlooked the green. Intellectuals, writers and liberal thinkers were also drawn to the area: Mary Wollstonecraft, the eighteenth-century feminist writer, had taught for a while in a building next to the chapel. The free-thinking Dissenters were on opposite sides of the green from the Mildmay evangelicals, however – in more ways than one.

In the August, the Taylors did manage to get away as a family. Jennie escaped first with the three children – to 'lodgings' in Hastings on the south coast. Hudson was delayed on speaking engagements in the North. Jennie pleaded with him to decline extra meetings – 'it will not pay to kill yourself, even to get the 100'. Eventually he arrived, utterly spent, but was gone again after three or four precious days. Jennie, staying on with the children for a few more days, wrote to him: 'I wonder whether God will ever give us the little time of family life alone.'

Hastings itself proved an ideal location, and the family holidayed there the following year when Hudson was away. Millie and Ernie found it excellent for going off 'adventuring'; Amy preferred a book at home. While there, Jennie received visits from her sister, Nellie, who with her husband, Charles, was still based in London. Even her brother Alfred came for a rare visit.

Meanwhile, in America a Mr and Mrs Frost were applying to join the Mission. There were health issues, however, and the time was not right for them, but their enthusiasm didn't stop there. Why shouldn't the CIM open a branch on their side of the Atlantic, so other Americans could respond to 'China's claim'? In the November, Henry Frost decided to press his case: he set sail to come and see Hudson Taylor.

At first, Hudson was not supportive of this proposal; but he did accept an invitation to speak in the United States the following year; it fitted in with a similar invitation he had received from his evangelist friend Mr Moody for around the same time.

During March 1888, on this side of the Atlantic, Hudson's ongoing itinerary extended to the Continent. Again, Jennie accompanied him; but first, courtesy of the Bergers, they had nearly a week's rest in Cannes. Refreshed from genteel company in spring warmth – and time alone together – they set out on the speaking tour, which included Genoa and San Remo in northern Italy, then into Switzerland via the new Alpine St Gotthard railway tunnel, at the time the longest tunnel in the world. Their Swiss engagements started in Lausanne on beautiful Lake Geneva, and went on from there. This was Jennie's first visit to Switzerland, and as with Hudson on his first visit, she found it exhilarating. They returned to London on 7 April. Some of their Continental audiences had been English-speaking, but they were also becoming acclimatised to the staccato style of speaking required for interpretation.

Later in 1888, Maria and Joe were married in China. Then also later that year Charles started his classics degree at Cambridge; he was reaping the benefit, as with his older brothers, of his excellent educational grounding.

Then came the promised journey to the US and Canada; Hudson sailed from Liverpool on 23 June, accompanied by his newly qualified doctor son Howard, Mr Radcliffe, an evangelist friend – and Mrs Radcliffe! Jennie was glad it was not hers to choose whether to go or stay. Anyway, a multitude of responsibilities back in London rather indicated she would be more fulfilled at home. America meant little to her at this stage, although she did realise that Hudson would be going straight on, from America's West Coast, to her beloved China. There were certainly no hard feelings between the wives, and she and Mrs Radcliffe enjoyed a good correspondence.

All three of the remaining children were sensitive to Jennie's needs and loss, helping with the work while 'Papa' was in America; Millie was getting to grips with the new 'writing machine'. And coincidentally on 26 June Hudson executed his first typewritten letter to Jennie. He was delighted his on-board correspondence was no longer at the mercy of the swell.

It was a phenomenal itinerary. Hudson settled well to the epic train journeys, some on his own, taking him from New York north to other cities, then across to Buffalo where he entered Canada. From here he went north-east as far as Montreal, before returning back into the States, this time travelling 'out West' to Kansas and Omaha, then back into Canada and across the entire vast breadth of the continent, stopping night after night for meetings, finally reaching Vancouver. The beauty of Niagara Falls and the Rockies was not wasted on him, but neither was the staggering response in the meetings. There was almost an embarrassment of giving, but much was in support of Americans and Canadians who were flocking forward to volunteer, with the implication they would go with the CIM. Hudson had to recognise God's leading concerning the extension of the Mission base on the other side of the Atlantic. Would there have to be a North American Council after all?

Howard had to return home to a new post at the London Hospital. Hudson sailed to China from Vancouver, taking fourteen new recruits, mainly Canadians, with him. They reached Shanghai on the last day of October.

Hudson's time in China was largely taken up, as ever, with personnel problems. Time was also spent deliberating with John Stevenson and others about the new North American Council. What exactly would its relationship be to both the London and China councils? Again there were communication problems with London: the resulting differences of opinion felt horrendous. Jennie talked to Benjamin Broomhall (who at one point felt he should resign over the matter). She wrote to Hudson asking if it would not be better if the US mission were separate, with CIM support where possible.

In April 1889 Hudson set off to come home – as much as anything to sort the 'American question' out. Back in London, again communicating in the same room, the atmosphere cleared. The North American Council of the CIM would be established, would function independently but on CIM principles, and would deal directly with China. Hearts were united in thankfulness that God had granted this amazing step forward.

Later that year, in the July, Hudson returned for a very short visit to North America. He was there for a month, in which time it was decided to site the new council HQ in Toronto, Canada. Henry Frost should be the undoubted chairman, so the Frosts willingly moved from the States to Canada.

With transport limited to boats and trains, and the well-established transatlantic telegraph system efficient but by nature superficial, would the whole enterprise work? No other missionary society had an international base at this time.

After his latest trip to China, Hudson had again met Jennie in Paris. This was proving such an excellent way of avoiding the otherwise very public reunion.

But how long would they have to keep meeting like this? The years of separation were at last coming to an end. Jennie's next foreign rendezvous with her husband would be in China.

19

'I Do Not Get Sea-sick but Heart-sick' (1889–94)

Hudson Taylor was ahead of his time in his attitude to both the importance and the capabilities of female workers. But it had never really occurred to the CIM leadership, or to men in general for that matter, that women could be valuable in decision-making. For the CIM, the beginnings of change came with the establishment of a Ladies Council. Its powers would be limited, of course, but there was a need for the careful assessment of the increasing numbers of female candidates (numerically now exceeding men), and this if nothing else would be much better handled by experienced women. The make-up of the council was generally predictable: Mrs Theodore Howard, Mrs Benjamin Broomhall, Mrs Hudson Taylor . . . clearly chosen for their husbands' worth, as well as their own undoubted talents. But there was one surprise inclusion: Miss Henrietta Soltau – a name from the past.

Henrietta's responsibilities for running the home for missionary children (generally non-CIM) were coming to an end. Hudson Taylor invited her to consider returning to Pyrland Road, to take on the eventual leadership of a female candidates' home.

The home was set up at 41 Pyrland Road. It was the joyful yet serious task of Jennie and her Ladies Council team to fill it with appropriate female candidates.

The Ladies Council was first convened on 23 September 1889. They functioned well, not only in their responsibilities, but there were times of crisis and challenge when they and the London Council had important times of prayer together.

For Jennie's forty-sixth birthday on 6 October, she and Hudson visited her father, now moved out to the leafy market town of Tenterden in the heart of the Kentish Weald. He had remarried, Ann, nine years younger than he, and the family had taken her to their hearts. They called her Grandma, alongside Grandpa, and the younger Taylor children, as well as Nellie's large brood, often went down to stay. On Sundays Mr and Mrs Faulding rode their carriage along Tenterden High Street to the newly rebuilt Zion Baptist Chapel. And Tenterden was just inland from Hastings, so they took their holidays with the family there also.

At the end of 1889 it was time for another short visit to Europe, this time to Scandinavia; Hudson took Howard with him on this hectic speaking tour of Sweden, Norway and Denmark, and they shared the itinerary. The meetings were amazing, with a massive response everywhere, both financial and personal. Individual Swedes were already in China as associates of the CIM. From now on the Swedish Mission in China would become an associate mission.

It was about to be the CIM's season for welcoming many associate societies.

While travelling together, Hudson and Howard began to talk about Charles: now in his second year at Cambridge he was causing concern. Hudson wrote to Jennie that Howard was corresponding with his brother 'prayerfully'. Charlie could be so easily led the wrong way, he said to Jennie.

Scandinavia took so much out of him that on their return Hudson was unwell and totally incapacitated until after Christmas. Time and again his hosts around the world wanted to pay for first-class travel for their honoured speaker, to enable him to rest on his return journey; he rarely accepted. Jennie had plenty to do while Hudson recovered, however, including her work with *China's Millions*. She now had almost complete editorial responsibility: Broomhall, preoccupied with other work, was happy to just glance through. The official editor was still Hudson, even if on the other side of the world; and he could be exacting, sending Jennie a long list of small changes each time.

Another pleasant distraction for Jennie at this time was the laying of the foundation stone of the 'new' Mildmay Mission Hospital nearby, by their friend Lady Tankerville. (Continuing her valued support of the CIM, she also later donated a 'Norwegian chalet', dismantled and moved from their estate, and re-sited in the Kent countryside. Well into the twentieth century it was a blessing to many as a holiday home, and briefly as a children's hostel.) The elderly and much-loved Mrs Pennefather, one half of the partnership which had originally been responsible for founding the Mildmay Mission, died two years later. Hudson was honoured to be invited to give the main address at the memorial service of this close friend.

On 17 March 1890, Hudson again left for China. Howard too had decided to commit himself long-term to the work in China. His father wanted him out more quickly, however, as Maria's first baby was due, and he wasn't sure any other medical person would be around to help. So Howard had sailed in the January. Unbeknown to Hudson and Jennie, this would be their last angst-ridden parting from each other.

On 27 April, Hudson reached Shanghai, keenly anticipating his first sight of the newly completed Wusong Road premises. He found a welcoming mission home and plenty of office space all built round a grassy quadrangle. For weary travellers from distant parts, how welcome would clean bedsheets be now, after nights spent on unswept floors of vermin-infested inns?

The Second China Inter-Mission Conference was to be held in the May. This one took place in a Shanghai theatre – and Hudson was responsible for the opening address. To much agreement and acclaim, he called for growth in the entire missionary community; employing his missionary maths he demonstrated clearly what 1,000 new recruits could achieve within five years.

There was much agreement also on other wide-ranging topics, but the vexed problem of attitudes to ancestor worship was re-aired, and again remained unresolved.

A near disaster occurred at the end of the conference. The more than four hundred delegates were assembled on a bank of seating for a group photo, when the structure collapsed and those in the centre landed one on top of another. Thankfully there was no serious injury and no panic, largely due to the patience of those who for a while were trapped underneath. The photographer had the presence of mind to keep photographing, and eventually a picture of the collapsed structure – minus the people – appeared in *China's Millions*. Hudson sent two pictures home to Jennie. She in turn was reporting favourably to Hudson on the increasingly international make-up of the Pyrland Road prayer meetings, since the developing European connections. It brought a new excitement to the meetings, she said, and she loved seeing Russians, Germans, Finns and Swedes chatting to each other afterwards in various languages, over cups of tea.

Howard Taylor became engaged to Geraldine Guinness in May 1890; she had joined the CIM and arrived in China in January 1888. In fact, Howard had been secretly sweet on her since childhood, when the Guinnesses and Taylors first encountered each other in Dublin and London. He had been very patient, receiving at least one rebuff. At 26, Geraldine was mature, experienced in work amongst the poor of London, and remarkably gifted in speaking and writing; she and Jennie were destined to become very close. Hudson's other son, Herbert, with Jeanie had had a baby son, Hudson's first grandchild. Maria and Joe were also expecting.

Then, just when Hudson Taylor seemed fully stretched in all directions, Australia beckoned.

'You will find many warm friends of the CIM to welcome you to Australia' was typical of the letters he was now receiving. With some already active in China, a provisional committee in place and plans for a training home and a permanent Australasian Council, their enthusiasm conveyed a sense of urgency, so in the July, Hudson sailed to Australia from Hong Kong. For Jennie at this stage, it just meant a new map to come to terms with, and limited knowledge of where her husband might be.

Separation from Jennie was getting unbearable for Hudson: 'I do not get sea-sick but heart-sick.' But he had had with him in China the three of his children who had successfully negotiated the adolescent years; Jennie was coping with the other end of the family, the four whose development was still a work in progress. They still needed her. Charlie was bringing unhelpful influences home from Cambridge. He was, apparently, 'far away from God'. For Ernie's part, could he perhaps receive favourable terms at the Leys School, in Charlie's footsteps? Ernie was turning out to be a bright pupil: '[he] deserves a better chance . . . dear boy!' Millie was now away at Addlestone, a town south-west of London, with a teaching post in a home for destitute female children. As for Amy, 'she needs keeping grace, for she is very emotional and loving'. 'I feel as if my heart would almost break if you don't come', wrote Hudson, 'but it would be altogether heart-breaking if any harm came to our dear children through my selfishness in taking you away. To die, alone, would be better than that!'

They discussed her bringing Ernie and Amy with her (at 15 and 13), but Ernie's schooling was too important. Perhaps they could stay with Grandpa Faulding, or with her brother William, who was now a 'retired preacher', and running a temperance hotel in Holborn. At least that would avoid Ernie leaving his education behind. There was so much still to settle – but just 'Hand over CM [*China's Millions*] to Charles Fishe' was Hudson's final desperate instruction.

Arriving in Darwin, Hudson then spoke in Brisbane, Sydney, Tasmania and Adelaide – and Melbourne, where the new headquarters would be. A huge crowd waved Hudson off outside Melbourne Town Hall when he left for Shanghai on 20 November, taking twelve new recruits with him. Jennie left London the day before, but with Hudson spending time in Brisbane and Darwin on the way home, she reached Shanghai before he did.

Back in Pyrland Road she would be missed now as the one who normally shared news from the field. 'When someone else rises to read the letters . . . lift your hearts to God for me, and say: "Make her a blessing to her husband; make her a blessing wherever she goes."'

They met again in Shanghai on 21 December. Never again would they be apart for so long, and at such a distance. She had been nine years away from China. The buildings along the Bund were taller and more sophisticated. The foreign concessions were dominant, model versions of small French, British or American cities. But as she travelled inland, she realised she had forgotten much: the dirty streets with pigs scavenging and their piglets tripping you up, the children with their bare bottoms, and the invasive but harmless curiosity of the women. With the exception of decapitated heads suspended by their pigtails, or the awful occasional standing cage, she remembered how much she loved it all. And she soon noticed how her presence seemed to double Hudson's already brimful capacity for and enjoyment of his work.

Even while still at the Yangchow training home, Geraldine Guinness was writing beautifully crafted articles for *China's Millions*. Hudson soon invited her to research and write the history of the Mission; basing herself in Shanghai, she started almost straight away. At Christmas they were a large company, from Canada, Europe and now Australia; satisfyingly like the make-up of the prayer meetings at home, Jennie observed. There was a sense of much blessing at this time; Jennie herself was riding high on encouragement and infectious enthusiasm. 'There is a real spirit of prayer and quickening in the Home here', she wrote.

Then on 17 February 1891, all at once, thirty-five Swedes burst on the scene – complete with guitars and exuberance. And in China, something had to be done quickly with all that blonde hair! They sung wherever they went, and filled the new headquarters with their singing. They taught new, catchy songs of praise, in English and Swedish. 'Faith set to music' was how Geraldine described them.

These were days of rapid growth. The CIM was now larger, consequently more conspicuous in China and more exposed to criticism. Communication and misunderstanding were always a challenge, particularly with three home councils. Delegation came hard to Hudson, as it had done to Moses. John Stevenson was doing well but sadly was worn down by family worries, and seeking to step down from oversight for a while.

Jennie was often in Shanghai while Hudson travelled, but this was easier than being oceans apart. She constantly wrote letters, answering Hudson's and keeping up with remote stations. Sometimes it was frustrating telling people he had changed his plans. She sent him occasional letters of mild reproof: he really should 'wire' his plans and whereabouts so she would know whether or not to forward items to him. She cared pastorally now for hundreds of workers. 'Counselling', of course, was unknown; particularly in a marriage, and particularly when addressing an aggrieved wife, the advice was very much not to rock the boat. But with her loving support and spiritual advice, most situations appeared to resolve.

Meanwhile in March, Geraldine received an urgent call to return home for a month, to look after her mother. She was still not married. Howard was still a patient man. Also that month a letter arrived for the Taylors from a well-named Mr Wright, wanting to marry Millie. It was a good letter, so they advised the couple become better acquainted with each other: she was now of an age to make up her own mind. And as the time to return home again approached, the Taylors decided to travel via Canada, to consult on the 'councils' challenge with the ever-wise Henry Frost.

They left Shanghai on 10 May 1892 to cross the Pacific. The journey started well, heading north through the beautiful Nagasaki Bay – but in all, it was a trying journey to Vancouver; they were both unwell, Hudson particularly, and it was not a good cabin. The exhilarating rail journey across Canada was far more refreshing, and Frost's wisdom on the vexed problem of managing three councils was invaluable. They arrived in Liverpool on 26 July – perfect timing for Hudson to take the platform at Keswick. Ernie and Amy were there to meet them at the convention, and afterwards Hudson took Amy with him to fulfil engagements in the North.

Back in London, there were ongoing and heated deliberations concerning the three councils. At times it felt like a stressful stalemate – but then to Jennie's delight particularly, Henry Frost came on a return visit from Canada. After getting to know him so well in Toronto, she believed his wisdom and experience would somehow lead to a resolution. It was unanimously agreed that the China Council would indeed remain in supreme charge, and the UK, North American and soon the Australasian Council would each relate directly to China, not to the UK. To Hudson Taylor this had always seemed right, but for some at home, feeling responsible for the people they were sending to an 'unknown' land, it did take some adjustment.

Meanwhile, Benjamin Broomhall was pushing himself. He was involved in the fight against Britain's iniquitous opium trade with China, as well as championing other social causes. These passions would last until the end of his life, but now in his sixties he was growing deaf, and struggling with the work of the CIM Home Council. Hudson's stop-gap remedy was to appoint a deputy for him on the Council, a Mr Sloane, just returned with his wife after showing great promise in China. It was agreed on the Council it was good to have someone with first-hand experience of China. Benjamin officially retired in January 1895, and Walter Sloane took over as senior general secretary. John Stevenson had also come home for a much-needed break, and to cope with his multiple family concerns. William Cooper took over from him as Hudson's deputy in China.

By May 1893, the building of the new headquarters was beginning on the land to the rear of Inglesby House; Inglesby itself was retained, continuing to be used for male candidates. Hudson explained in a letter that the builders were actually opening up a former path for access through the Inglesby coach house to the gardens and new premises at the rear. Here there would be thirty bedrooms, plus meeting rooms, and an abundance of office space.

Meanwhile, Hudson was again travelling throughout the UK. Sometimes he would sit to preach, and naturally this concerned Jennie. Yet if she expressed this, he didn't like it: 'You should trust God' – in spite of the often desperate tone of his letters inviting her concern. She walked a tightrope. He had the amazing ability to recover so quickly after complete collapse, seemingly with no awareness of how it may affect those who cared.

Jennie was glad that Hudson took a particular interest in Amy, their youngest, who by her retiring nature could otherwise miss out. In April, he took her with him to Germany, her first trip abroad. After she had recovered from mild sea-sickness, she thoroughly enjoyed the experience of airing her schoolgirl German. Millie, still with the East in her blood, was travelling to India as the newlywed Mrs Wright. 'Our pets are grown', wrote Hudson. 'We must pray that God will help our children to be far more to Him than ever we have been.' But: 'I hope God will help us about Charlie.'

Geraldine Guinness was released from her home responsibilities in February 1894; to her delight, she would be returning to China with the Taylors, of whom she was becoming increasingly fond. They sailed to New York, and all three spoke at various engagements across the US, including the significant Student Convention in Detroit – where Geraldine's noted ability to hold a young audience had a remarkably stirring effect. Eventually they reached San Francisco, and from there set sail to China. Sunny California was a new experience for all of them; since the recent Gold Rush, and arrival of the railway, San Francisco was now almost as sophisticated as New York; a friend paid for the three to stay in the America-sized luxurious Occidental Hotel – and great joy, San Francisco had a significant Chinese community.

They reached Shanghai on 17 April; here the Taylors would be based for the next two years.

Howard was waiting in Shanghai for the arrival of his bride – and they were married in the cathedral on 24th. Following their honeymoon on a houseboat on the Grand Canal, almost immediately they became concerned about their 'parents', who were planning to travel to Shansi, the province of extremes. And summer was the worst time for travel, with either burning sun or drenching rain. The 'parents', of course, were not concerned about themselves, but about others, namely some Scandinavians who were getting into difficulties there, as a result of which some female workers were in a vulnerable position. So, a party of five set off inland (the newlyweds, Hudson and Jennie, and son-in-law Joe, Maria and her little ones having just left for the UK). They went as far as they could by boat, then it was wheelbarrows, then finally the two-mule carts, all in impossible heat. For Hudson and Jennie, the seniors of the party, it was no easier for the fact they had done it before. The malodorous sweat of the drivers and the discordant but infuriatingly rhythmical squeak of the wheels seemed worse this time. At night, Geraldine and Jennie (whom Geraldine called 'Mother') slept in rooms hardly fit for animals, with vermin for company; the men of the party often slept outside in the carts, sometimes to the accompaniment of mules enjoying a noisy fight. Jennie, with her positive take on things, wrote home about everything from the splendour of Sian, Shensi's ancient capital, to the excitement of discovering so many new stations and little church gatherings. Here they were supplied with modest provisions for the onward journey: apricots, persimmons, walnuts, spiced water-melon . . . and delicious sweetmeats always wrapped in red paper.

They crossed into Shansi, where the brilliant, tragic poppy fields waved tauntingly. After a conference at Pingyang (of the 'famine' monument) they were welcomed for a while into the home of a man already celebrated in missionary circles, the one-time Confucian scholar known as Pastor Hsi. Delivered from opium addiction and idol worship, he was now a leading Christian, a true trophy of God's grace. Well-educated, cultured and with a gentle manner, with his wife he was now running several opium refuges, seeing others delivered from addiction by prayer, and occasional medicine. He had longed for this day, when Mr and Mrs Taylor would honour them with their presence; along with the rest of their party, they were now served a feast of good food, after which they were conducted to specially prepared visitors' quarters, a suite of rooms adapted from a barn, but newly furnished with colourful hangings, clean white towels, fresh floor coverings, and lamps burning warmly. Hsi himself brought in their hot water. ('How could I do less?')

After Hudson was satisfied problems in Shansi were resolved, they set off from Taiyuen, on the long journey out to Tientsin on the coast; again, it was a route they had both taken before. Even in September the heat was still impossible, and the party took to sleeping in the day, and travelling by night – a common practice in that part of the world.

The midnight meal was often what they had brought with them on the carts – not easy to assemble by moonlight. The drama of the journey climaxed when they had to cross a swollen river. The mules panicked midstream and became unharnessed from their litters, leaving passengers inside in imminent danger of drowning. The two ladies were trapped. For a minute, watching the water rising inside their litter, there seemed no hope, but the muleteers reached them just in time, leaving them with no more than a soaking.

Jennie and Geraldine, of different generations, were nevertheless drawn together in their journeying, with their shared dangers and sleeping arrangements. On top of everything else, Geraldine while travelling had suffered two miscarriages – the only hope, as it turned out, of her ever having children. Although not easy, Jennie was able to support her through private sorrow into an eventual strong place of faith and acceptance. The little party had been four months on the road.

Could they have had any idea of Shansi's fate still to come?

Back in Shanghai, but with war between China and Japan, largely over Korea, now declared, the effect on Hudson was to increase his desire to remain in China. Jennie became more and more his amanuensis. Day after day she wrote to Mr Stevenson, in England with his family, but needing updating on events in China: '[We are] needing to be much in prayer as sh^d the Japs get to Pekin one cannot tell what might follow'.

There was an armistice – but China was beginning to lose face next to a modernising Japan. Would they take their embarrassment and anger out on scapegoats? Would Christians be among the usual suspects? China's future leader, the young and yet-to-be-discovered Sun Yat-Sen, saw the signs – and fled to London. Hudson began to warn the CIM of possible dangers to come.

20

The Penny Had Dropped at Last (1895–98)

After nineteen years and accompanied by five of their ten children, Charles and Nellie Fishe returned to China in 1895; they would remain in Shanghai involved in administration and other work at Wusong Road. Jennie, of course, was delighted to have her sister with her in China once more – not that she saw much of her. She and Hudson were travelling up the Yangtze to a conference in Chungking, when Jennie had to stop at Yangchow with a severely infected foot.

By mid-July, Jennie and Hudson were both at Chefoo, in recovery mode again, Hudson hardly able to sit up due to neuralgia. But as ever, the bracing Chefoo air worked its magic, and Hudson plunged straight into details of plans for more school buildings. He never wanted to be too far removed from his sense of responsibility for the Chefoo schools. The following year, the foundation stone was laid for the new boys' school building. The school was thriving and expanding, registered as a centre for sitting the

The Penny Had Dropped at Last (1895–98) 223

College of Preceptors pupils' exams – and immediately getting excellent marks. It was definitely in the running now for the coveted unofficial 'Best School East of Suez' title. Mr Frank McCarthy, son of the McCarthys who had been with Jennie in Hangchow, took over the headship, a post he would retain for thirty-five years. The next generation were returning, whatever their parents had suffered.

It had been an encouraging year, albeit with some setbacks. There had been church growth, and the goal for the 'Thousand' new missionaries had been exceeded, across forty-five different societies.

As if the Taylors, veterans now of some truly epic travelling, had not done enough, an invitation suddenly came from a completely different direction. Calcutta was hosting the last in a series of Student Volunteer Movement Conferences held across India; would Hudson Taylor accept an invitation to be the main speaker? He realised this could be combined with a visit to one of CIM's extreme outposts, in Tibet. Hudson had been in correspondence with the general secretary of the Tibetan Pioneer Mission, who also happened to be on CIM's London Council; there were some critical leadership challenges in his Mission, and he knew how valuable a visit from Hudson Taylor could be. It was pointed out to Hudson that the station was near the Indian border: 'If you could [underlined] go to Kalimpong to see them all' was the general secretary's urgent plea. As it happened, Hudson had also heard from one of the leaders themselves, a pioneering single lady who had been a member of the CIM.

So, on 18 January 1896, the Taylors set out by ship for India. Finance had been given specifically for Jennie to accompany her husband, but they gave most of it away, choosing rather to travel in third-class accommodation. This involved separate sleeping compartments, but they worked it so that their doors were adjoining.

The Port of Calcutta with its clamorous dockside trade and backstreet slums held no surprises for the Taylors. But while there, their hosts took them to see what the tourists see, and they were shown the now somewhat sanitised site of the famous Black Hole. They were even conducted as far as Agra, with its glorious Taj Mahal, taking in Benares on the way. In India, unlike China, railways took you anywhere. And everywhere they were impacted by Hinduism, and its effects particularly on the poor. After the Student Conference, they set out on their second quest. They thoroughly enjoyed the final stages of their journey, on one of India's sturdy narrow-gauge railways. Climbing up and up through tea plantation terraces, they eventually reached Darjeeling, with the snow-clad Himalayas in the distance. Even here, and in nearby Kalimpong, they discovered western colonialism had left its architectural mark; at least in China it stopped at the coast! Here they met with the members of the struggling Tibetan Pioneer Mission (which later became the Tibetan Mission Band, and applied to be an associate mission of CIM). After a hopefully worthwhile time of advice and encouragement, on 10 March the Taylors returned to Shanghai.

They left China once more in the May, to travel back to England. Having just come as usual through the Suez Canal, they disembarked this time in Brindisi in southern Italy. They were then escorted on something of a grand tour through Italy, before the final and more familiar leg of their journey. They were looking forward to their first sighting of the brand-new Newington Green headquarters. The offices had actually relocated from Pyrland Road just over a year before, and 6 Pyrland Road had been sold.

They knew they would be arriving home on a Saturday evening, but it was not their intention to disrupt the regular prayer meeting. Amy had a rough idea of the arrival time of the Dover train, and she and others rushed between Charing Cross and Cannon Street stations in an effort to meet her parents. Their train had pulled in to St Paul's Station, however, from where, giving everyone the slip, they took a hansom to arrive without any fuss. It dropped them on Newington Green, and they walked down the private road that led through Inglesby – and there framed against the evening sunlight was the new building. They walked through the door with 'Have Faith in God' etched above it, then settled quietly at the back of the prayer meeting, deferring greetings, kisses and much acclaim until the end. Hudson insisted on a detailed tour before he retired for the night; all was entirely as he had planned and anticipated – except the cellars, which he said were far too small to accommodate quantities of cheap out-of-season coal!

Mail was soon arriving addressed to 'CIM Home, Newington Green'. Hudson himself used that address when writing from Salisbury in September. He was on a speaking tour, accompanied by Ernest. Later in the month he was in Europe again, with engagements in Germany and throughout Scandinavia; he was in a different city nearly every night. He still wrote passionately to Jennie, even when, as he said, they were only a day apart. He was glad to hear that she was 'getting near Charlie' – so all was not lost with his wayward son.

There were more speaking engagements throughout the UK that autumn, and Hudson took Amy. He wrote from Edinburgh to Jennie, who was in Hastings with her father, suggesting she join them in Edinburgh. The Scottish October chill had taken him by surprise: could she bring his warmer socks, and a thicker travel blanket? On one trip (and surprisingly for those acquainted with his generous and most un-Chinese beard), he wrote: 'I find I have not got my razor. I shaved with a surgical inst[rument]!'

In the spring, Hudson set off on yet another speaking tour, this time with Walter Sloan. On the road (or rather, rail) for more than two months, often spending just one or two nights in each place, they travelled through France, Germany, Austria, then Switzerland, with speaking engagements in city after city. Some congregations heard him in English, but speaking predominantly via interpreter with the discipline of having to speak in bite-size chunks, added to the strain. Postcards to Jennie usually arrived daily; privacy being an issue with postcards, Hudson lapsed almost entirely into Romanised (probably Ningpo) Chinese.

By the end of July, yet another wealthy friend was insisting they take a break in Davos, in order for Hudson to recover from this latest exhausting speaking tour. It was an oft-repeated pattern of extreme exertion, complete collapse and rapid recovery. They were placed in the plush surroundings of the Hotel d'Angleterre, at that time the only building of any size in the Davos-Platz valley. But as Hudson gained strength once more, Jennie fell and sprained her right wrist – so neither of them could write letters. As often happens in those circumstances, replies eventually slowed also – so for a while it was a complete break. They needed

The Penny Had Dropped at Last (1895–98)

to be well refreshed, as there would be shocking news for each of them by the end of the summer.

First, while still in Switzerland they heard that on 23 August, Jennie's sister, Nellie, had died suddenly in China. She was only 46. Her husband Charles was left alone with their five youngest children. Jennie made plans to hurry home to comfort her bereaved father; Hudson had business to see to in Sweden. But incredibly the same day they received a letter from Maria saying she had just lost her latest newborn to dysentery. Then a week or so later came more. In London, Jennie received the agonising news that Maria herself had also died of dysentery, on 28 September, so not long after her baby. She was just 30. Her father, Hudson, was unaware, and currently sailing from Sweden to Edinburgh. Jennie immediately wrote to their contacts in Edinburgh asking if she could come and stay, in order to break the news personally to Hudson. On his eventual arrival, Jennie's unexpected presence in Edinburgh, as well as her demeanour, immediately foretold critical news. Personal sacrifice continued unrelenting.

The coming weeks were indeed difficult for both of them; concentration eluded them at times; the days of the funerals, so far away, were a particular trial. 'The Lord has helped us thro' such a time as I never remember', Jennie wrote in a letter.

Both husbands, grieving heavily and left with young children, nevertheless remarried within a couple of years, as was the almost universal habit of male missionaries who were widowed young.

In November 1897, the Taylors left for what would be Jennie's sixth visit to China. It was thought it would be the final one in active service for them both. They were going via the United States, and this time they were taking Henrietta Soltau with them.

There were many in Pyrland Road who achieved so much for China – but only Henrietta took what later became the popular short-term trip. She had never travelled before, but it was generally agreed it would be invaluable, her life's work now being preparing others for China.

In the early days of the voyage, however, there was some unexpected strain; the independent Henrietta, the same age as Jennie but thoroughly accustomed to her single lifestyle, found it challenging to be organised and told what to do. Jennie, who still had the ability to find fun and laughter in the adaptability which travel required, found this strange at first. The seasoned travellers hardly noticed the routine requirement outside New York harbour to anchor at the quarantine station. But this, and so much else both in New York, and later in San Francisco, left Henrietta confused and bewildered.

On 15 January they reached Shanghai, and Henrietta's uncomfortable induction period was coming to an end. She set off on her tour of the inland stations, addressing gatherings wherever she went. She was reunited with many who remembered her from Pyrland Road, and was a great blessing everywhere. Additionally, the privations of travel in China when it came to it seemed to suit her better than the luxury of the US 'railroad'. She dressed, ate and travelled like the Chinese. A year later she returned to London. Her 'trip of a lifetime' had the anticipated totally positive effect on her work with candidates.

Also in London, Ernest, having qualified as an accountant, was preparing to join most of the rest of his family in China. His heart was set on pioneering. He arrived in Shanghai while his parents were there. And Howard and Geraldine left for Australia in October 1898 – for a rest, but also with the inevitable speaking engagements.

Through most of 1898, the CIM was facing a new challenge, and wherever the Taylors happened to be, they needed to be updated. For some years, a wealthy Christian businessman (living on his Mediterranean yacht for much of the year) had been giving to the CIM. He was particularly committed to supporting schools work and to training Chinese church workers. In September 1897 he died suddenly, leaving an enormous and unprecedented sum to the Mission, to be paid in instalments. But complications developed when his will was contested by his sons, and litigation was threatened. If the benefactor for whatever reason had not provided for his immediate family, that would be considered, by the Mission at least, as unrighteous behaviour; but on the other hand, if he had prayerfully fully intended to bring blessing in a particular direction by his bequest, it would be unfaithful of the CIM, they felt, to refuse or redirect it. Exhausting sometimes trans-global telegraphic and written discussions went on for months on the subject. All was resolved eventually, however, without recourse to the law, and the draughts started arriving.

In November 1898, the Taylors were yet again on the Yangtze, travelling upriver to the West China Inter-Missions Conference in Chungking – and this time they got there. It was not straightforward, however; the long journey of hundreds of miles could often take three months, and involved three different kinds of vessel. First there was the stocky steamer, then the native houseboat, still with comfortable living accommodation on-board; in places here houses were built out over the water, toddlers were tied securely on long leashes allowing them to play on balconies, and human and other household waste was jettisoned straight down holes into the river. The final mode of transport was the specially designed Szechwan junk, strong and light for negotiating the fearsome rapids along the most breath-taking part of the gorge. Not all boats were successful, to which wrecks along the way paid silent testimony. Other potential disasters were averted by the remarkably adept bright-red lifeboats, a rare professional public service. Here the sides of the gorge often rose sheer for several hundred feet, and in places the boats must be towed; the passengers walked, the path having been blasted out of the cliffs either side, while the mighty Yangtze crashed and foamed below.

While they were in Chungking, they learned from the leader of the work in that region about another example of incredible largesse. He and his wife had recently entertained a most unusual guest.

Fearless international explorer, best-selling travel writer and household name Isabella Bird had turned up one day on the mission's doorstep. The first female Fellow of the Royal Geographical Society – so fellow Fellow with Hudson Taylor – she wrote detailed, almost forensic, descriptions of everywhere she went. This meant she was fascinating company, but somewhat time-consuming as she asked so many questions. In recent years she had suffered the loss of both her husband, after only five years of an otherwise happy marriage, and her dearly loved sister. And now, with her considerable private means, she was intent on memorialising them in the poorest parts of the world. She was totally supportive of Christian missionary work, especially that of hospitals. Having already funded two hospitals in India, she quickly found a suitable building near the CIM station in Szechwan; in next to no time, the Henrietta Bird Memorial Hospital was founded, complete with future provision for running costs.

The rigors of the trip were too much for Hudson once again. This time he almost died with bronchitis. Jenny knew he was now incapable of any travel, whether by boat or cart, unless accompanied at all times by a missionary, or a close Chinese friend.

They spent a peaceful early summer at Chefoo. The penny had dropped at last: Hudson could do no more, even in the face of political storm clouds gathering. Jennie was doing all the letter-writing, including the long updates to Mr Stevenson. As the camera and developing equipment came out again, she breathed a sigh of relief: it meant her husband was relaxing into recovery mode. And they were invited to join staff and pupils for some school social events, including a moonlit musical evening in one of the quadrangles, and later the Chefoo Foundation Day Games.

They also had time to travel south along the coast to visit Hangchow again. This was wonderful for Jennie, being the place where she had established so much. Her home for five years, it had been all she knew of China, yet she had been deeply content. Thirty years on – and Pastor and Mrs Wang were still there! And there were others who remembered her, the young Miss Happiness, stepping cheerily in and out of their homes.

The Taylors even planned a retirement cottage, two days' boat ride inland from Shanghai, where Hudson had bought a plot when it was cheap. It would be just two or three rooms, plus servants' quarters. They could even have a verandah looking out over the distant hills. This would be the only permanent home they had ever planned, let alone occupied. Was there a possibility perhaps neither would live to see it? Was it really the lifestyle they sought, anyway?

21

A Mantle of Horror (1899–1903)

On 7 August (1899) Jennie wrote: 'my husband is better, and I am alright again'. It was time to fulfil their promised return (or in Jennie's case, first visit) to Australasia. Sailing from Hong Kong, they arrived in Brisbane, joining the ever-peripatetic Howard and Geraldine, who had been there now almost a year. Hudson and Jennie had not in some ways wanted to leave China when they did, having some sense of troubles to come. Rumours of violence against foreigners were growing; but if persecution came, the Chinese Christians would always be the most vulnerable. Yet there was tremendous growth in numbers and maturity among the Chinese churches – the self-propagating aspect which Hudson so often missed out of his maths.

Jennie's letters betrayed a hint of finality on leaving China. If they had delayed it would have been harder to get away, but Hudson actually had in his sights an important meeting in New York the following April.

From Brisbane they travelled throughout Australia, with meetings in a different city almost every day. Jennie,

Howard and Geraldine shared Hudson's preaching load. The relatively new Australasian *China's Millions* gave a detailed report of Jennie's address to a large congregation in Melbourne. Fresh from her recent visit to Hangchow, it was easy for her to recall the incredible freedom she had known there for sharing the gospel with the women. She spoke with simple passion on how in every home she entered there had been a crowd waiting to listen. She believed the way had been prepared by faithful supporting prayer.

In every location, the foursome received generous hospitality. In Queensland they found themselves staying in the comfortable home of a sugar cane plantation owner. Then it was on to Tasmania, where on a hot Christmas Day they contemplated what the coming year might bring.

They crossed to New Zealand's South Island on 5 January 1900, journeying first to Christchurch for a week of meetings. They then crossed Cook Strait to North Island, for a nine-day hectic speaking schedule (thankfully again shared among the four) in Wellington. Here they were given a very special treat, and taken to see the Rotorua Hot Springs, courtesy of the UK government. Jennie had thought it was only the upper classes who toured the sights – or attractions, as they would soon be called. Overawed with the privilege, she made the most of every aspect, even down to the pungent sulphuric smell! She enjoyed the friendliness of the Maori people, noting every detail in a letter to Amy, who had been spending Christmas with friends in Germany.

Their deadline of April in New York was approaching; it was time to steam across the Pacific once again. It would be Jennie's fourth time of working out whether to add or miss a day as they crossed the Dateline.

A Mantle of Horror (1899–1903) 235

On 5 April the rocky hulk of Alcatraz came into view: it was the island fort and military prison which loomed sentry-like over the entrance to San Francisco Bay. From here the trans-continental railroad cosseted them all the way to the heart of Manhattan, almost to the door of the Carnegie Hall itself.

Here there would be several thousand gathering for the week-long Ecumenical Foreign Missions Conference, at which Hudson was speaking. The build-up was on a grand scale, with Theodore Roosevelt, soon to become US president, invited to give the opening address. Facing his largest audience to date, Hudson's contribution was, as always, straightforward, compelling, and enthusiastically received.

If anyone had glanced at the foreign pages of the papers during the conference, they might have seen some alarming news breaking from China: and it included the word 'Boxer' for the first time. Boxer numbers were growing, apparently, centring on the province of Shansi. And the Dowager Empress was pouring out terrible anti-foreign invective.

The causes of the Boxer Rebellion were complex: they consisted of a smouldering mix of the beginnings of republicanism, the opium curse, repeated famines, foreign-built railways and telegraph lines upsetting the *feng-shui* (the sense of balance and orderliness deemed essential to the nation's spiritual well-being), and Catholic priests getting above themselves and behaving and dressing like mandarins. The Boxers themselves had started as a martial arts secret society. The Dowager Empress, keeping her nephew, the young reformist emperor, under house imprisonment, started issuing the Boxers with imperial edicts to kill foreigners; she was playing with fire as far as the foreign powers were concerned.

After the conference, the younger Taylors had to return to London, and Henry Frost now took responsibility for their parents. He conducted them on to Toronto in Canada for the North American Council meetings, to be held in Berger House, the new Canadian HQ. The Taylors' dear friend Mr Berger had died in January 1899, and almost half the cost of this much-needed building was met from his generous bequest.

They returned to the US on a night sleeper – but for Hudson everything was beginning to get too much. Since leaving China, they had been travelling virtually non-stop for nine months. Not wishing to disappoint their friends, however, by super-human effort he stood up to speak in Boston. Then something began to go wrong. Jennie's hands grew clammy: she gripped the sides of her chair as she realised with horror that Hudson had lost track, and was repeating himself. He had to be 'rescued' by the chairman. The schedule was immediately terminated, and Hudson and Jennie sailed for England. They were met in London by a very relieved Amy and Charlie.

As soon as they could (after prioritising a weekend with her father), the Taylors set off for a holiday in Davos. They stayed in the Hotel Concordia, originally a sanatorium for TB patients, now run as a small guest house by friends of theirs. Hudson agreed it was necessary as it would be the quickest way for him to get back to work! So began the familiar regime: botany, photography and long walks: he knew the formula for recovery. At 'very moderate expense' they were able to stay until after Christmas.

A Mantle of Horror (1899–1903)

Telegrams from Shanghai were beginning to sound ominous, but it seemed all in the CIM were safe. But not only could the internal telegraph in China be unreliable, to make matters worse, Hudson discovered they had left their CIM telegraph code book at home: cables were pretty meaningless without this. Jennie was left trying to describe to someone at home where they might find it, in order to send it on.

Even in late July, cables from Mr Stevenson in Shanghai gave no hint of what had actually already happened. But eventually the terrible facts did start to stutter through.

At first it was confusing. Hudson referred to a June letter: 'it seems ancient history now! Have the stations been abandoned?'

Inevitably the truth became clear, but because of Hudson's emotional state, Jennie began filtering and staggering the news – especially the telegrams, which she tended to digest on her own first.

Eventually they learned the worst had been over by the end of July; the day of the most terrible massacre was 9 July. On this day, Geraldine's brother and fellow missionary Dr Whitfield Guinness, working in Honan province, sent a message to Shanghai which was typical of many: 'premises totally destroyed, property lost, no official protection, missionaries six days in hiding, cannot escape yet. Guinness – please disseminate'. The CIM lost fifty-eight missionaries, and forty-six children. This was the greatest loss of all missions, with the exception of the Catholics. Throughout the missionary community, 113 were slaughtered in all. But greater losses still were among the Chinese Christians – who, of course, could not flee the country.

The worst affected province was Shansi, and the worst affected area in Shansi was Taiyuen, where dozens were beheaded in one afternoon. For some it was a quick death, for some not; torture and deprivation were also widespread. Crazed criminals, famine-starved peasants and disaffected troops were always happy to join the Boxers for plunder. They set fire to any buildings in Peking and Tientsin with the remotest link to foreigners or Christianity. It seemed as if all China were burning.

In the September, Queen Victoria, herself with only weeks to live, instructed Lord Salisbury to write in protest to the Chinese emperor. China felt deeply humiliated in the face of reprisals threatened by western powers who had lost subjects.

The news was cumulative in its devastating effect, and Hudson was beside himself with grief; Jennie was somehow holding on, to both her sanity and his. Hudson took long walks 'to tire his brain out'. Later, when Amy arrived: 'Amy and he went up a mountain.'

The news became more and more heart-rending as individual details became known. Hudson had believed God would always protect them. He also had a tendency to self-blame, a habit of looking inward as if there were more he could have done, as in times past when funds were short. Now he had to process the fact of his complete impotence. And as Jennie once proved years before, safe in Hangchow during the Yangchow riot, it is the worst frustration to be prevented from doing anything to help. She wrote on behalf of them both: 'Day and night our thoughts are with you all.'

The most prominent CIM leader to be martyred was William Cooper, Stevenson's co-director in China.

A Mantle of Horror (1899–1903)

Mr Stevenson himself felt it deeply. The full weight of responsibility seemed to be upon him like a mantle of horror. It lived with him until his own death at the end of the First World War.

By the September, the Taylors were sending typed letters – a sure sign that Howard and Geraldine had arrived. Hudson started asking his son if he thought he, Hudson, was well enough for them to return to China. He desperately wanted to bring comfort and encouragement. 'Some who have been spared have perhaps suffered even more than some of those taken.' This was undoubtedly so. They need not feel sorry for the martyred; they would have no memory now of their sufferings: 'They do not regret it now.'

Geraldine and Howard were a tremendous strength to their parents. Hudson was as free to be himself in front of them, as with anyone. Day after day, hardly knowing what he was doing, he paced up and down, while Geraldine quietly sat at a desk in the same room, writing her biography of Pastor Hsi. (Pastor Hsi had died in 1896. Those who knew him were glad he hadn't lived to die a violent death at the hands of the Boxers. His widow however survived and continued the good work among addicts.)

On 7 August, Hudson wrote momentously to Dixon Hoste, who had been one of the Cambridge Seven, asking him to take over as acting general director. Mr Hoste wrote back and declined immediately, saying it should rather be John Stevenson, who was in China as Hudson's representative: he should not be overlooked. He also wrote to Jennie, as he often did, saying he had neither the qualities nor qualifications; but Stevenson, on the other hand, was fully supportive of Mr Taylor's decision, and didn't feel at all overlooked.

In the October, Howard and Geraldine had to leave for America to speak at student gatherings again. Although sorely missed by the parents, they were reaching the peak of their amazingly fruitful ministry partnership, and needed to be released.

Then on 15 November, Hudson had another letter from Dixon Hoste, in which he said he would accept, as long as he had Mr Stevenson's support – which he did. By now, Hoste was married to the eldest Broomhall daughter, so a niece of Hudson. On the strength of this, when writing to the Taylors he always addressed them as Uncle and Aunt.

At this point Hudson, beginning to rally, wrote to say that everything must facilitate getting missionaries, especially females, out of northern China, withdrawing emergency funds if necessary. Any deposits in Chinese banks might be looted anyway 'in troublous times', or might be withheld if the atmosphere turned against missionaries. Everyone must get to Shanghai if possible; Chinese Christians would anyway be safer without foreigners around. Home leave must be offered to all. If Chefoo was unsafe, they must evacuate to Japan.

At the beginning of 1901 the Taylors, feeling the cold in Davos, decided to spend the next three months in Cannes near the newly widowed Mrs Berger. It was thought by helpful Davos friends that it would be easier for the Taylors if their luggage were sent separately – but it never arrived. Mrs Berger was impressed at the calmness with which the Taylors took this minor disaster, on top of what they had already suffered.

In April they took a brief trip home – to a kingdom grappling with its new Edwardian identity. Hudson and Jennie

A Mantle of Horror (1899–1903)

had already written to the bereaved; now they wished to greet those who had returned, as well as the relatives of those who had not. They soon learned that no bitterness had been expressed in any letters received from China. And in churches generally there was an almost immediate response from some who wished to take the martyrs' places.

They also spent time with Jennie's ageing father. His engineer's mind was still active, and ever contemplating new ideas: trains, he said, would one day run on electricity.

One of Mr Hoste's first responsibilities in the New Year was particularly sensitive: he had to consider the desire of some missionaries to return to the stations in Shansi. Hoste believed he should go in person – and he took his new assistant, a certain Ernest Taylor, with him. The two worked well together, Ernest writing most of Mr Hoste's letters. Many, therefore, were the letters he wrote to his own parents addressed to Dear Uncle or Aunt.

The returning party were greeted like royalty on their slow journey back to Taiyuen, so great was the Chinese sense of shame. They were met on the way by viceroys, governors and mandarins, all offering obsequious apologies. And their entry into the city happened to be 9 July 1901, the dreaded first anniversary of the massacre.

'Satan was let loose in Shansi last summer', wrote Mr Hoste, 'it has been convulsed from end to end' – first by Boxers, then by fear of foreign reprisal. The Boxers themselves had now either been killed, or had committed suicide, or were in hiding.

The plan was that the CIM would demand no reparations. Any compensation for life or injury would be refused. If offered for destroyed property, some perhaps might be accepted. Individuals were free to claim, but most did not. Mr Hoste submitted a claim, helped by Ernest the accountant, then informed the Chinese they would not be accepting it. He wanted his actions to speak of the forgiveness of Jesus. This all proved a wise decision, as it was observed that resentment grew in areas where compensation was pursued. And missionaries were painfully aware anyway of the iniquities perpetrated by Britain on China.

Mr Hoste conducted many funerals and memorial services; the Chinese officials were only too keen to provide some pomp and significance to these otherwise potentially distressing occasions. The 'Shansi experience' was a baptism of fire for the Taylors' youngest son – but somehow God drew him to that tragedy-scarred province, with a sense of love and compassion, and eventually it became his field.

In May 1901, the Taylors returned to Switzerland, this time to Geneva where the now invalid Mrs Berger had settled. But then by July it was too hot for them so they removed to the Chamonix Valley at the foot of Mont Blanc, just into France. In September Amelia, on one of her rare trips abroad, came with her son Benjamin to stay with the Taylors in Chamonix. Together they walked and climbed, until one day Hudson slipped and jarred his spine. With memories of all those years ago, when it was thought perhaps he would never walk again, he was confined to bed. Later he became concerned after a sense of weakness on one side, that he had suffered a slight stroke. Jennie knew these things had a habit of clearing up. 'We won't have so many stairs in Geneva', she somewhat dismissively wrote.

A Mantle of Horror (1899–1903)

They did return to Geneva, on the Swiss side of the Lake. But in October, Geneva felt damp. They were beginning to look a bit like the *nouveaux riches*, with multiple moves according to season. Jennie was only too aware, yet knew her husband could hardly cope with anything else. 'God has been gracious in getting us here', she wrote. 'We are in every way shielded and helped.'

They returned to London for the spring, and Amy came home for an Easter visit. She was currently teaching English in Itzehoe, northern Germany. They all took a trip to see Grandpa Faulding, still active and out every day, and Mrs Faulding.

But in London, it was realised, Hudson did too much work. By May 1902, and his 70th birthday, he was using a Bath chair when out and about. He seemed so frail, and Jennie, as ever, was concerned: they must return to Switzerland, out of most people's reach. Recognising his own frailty at last, he agreed to rent an apartment or *pension* in the village of Les Chevalleyres, a picture-book location amongst orchards and meadows, and still near Lake Geneva. In a house suitably named *La Paisible* they took two rooms with a balcony, and a glazed south-facing verandah. The rent included meals and 'help'. This was the nearest they ever came to having a settled home. Home for Hudson had always been wherever Jennie was.

With a month or so of mountain air, Hudson was soon strong again. They soon knew everyone, from neighbours, to the Count and Countess who lived in the mediaeval chateau at Blonay. They had long been comfortable enjoying the country house hospitality of upper-class friends. And all the time Jennie wrote letters, on behalf of both of them.

She wrote long missives to Mr Stevenson every few days, always with updates on Hudson's undulating health and ability-to-cope profiles. There was always the unspoken assumption that Jennie would outlive Hudson by many years; consequently the enquiries and concerns, to which she always responded, were about him, not her. Amy came to stay in July. 'Each time she visits us now it is so uncertain whether she will see her Father again.' She wrote to Millie to update her on her adopted father's progress. Millie was still in South India with her husband, a coffee plantation owner. Jennie always wrote faithfully to all the family, but Millie was not such a good correspondent. Jennie wanted to send another parcel, but was reluctant until she could be sure the last one had arrived.

In November, Henry Frost and Dixon Hoste called in at the same time as each other, travelling from opposite sides of the globe. In fact, 'calling in' on the Taylors had suddenly become a whole lot simpler. The 'Siberian route' was now on everyone's lips, and in everyone's correspondence. Jennie wrote excitedly that you could now get from London to Shanghai in an incredible seventeen days – 'and no tropics and no sea-sickness'. It terminated at Vladivostok, so there was just the comparatively short steamer trip from there down the coast.

Walter Sloane also came across from London, to join Messrs Hoste and Frost in a discussion on Hudson's permanent handover to Dixon. It was also agreed Mr Sloane would become assistant home director to Mr Howard. This was all a relief, not least to Jennie. It seemed no contentious issue could possibly get past such inspired appointees now, to reach Hudson. Jennie later wrote about Mr Hoste's subsequent visits that he generally asked about 'this and that', while Hudson shared his thoughts as he paced the room, 'not that he has said anything very special'!

It was a good Christmas – a German one according to Jennie, which she particularly liked. 'We had a pleasant ramble in the wood on Christmas day.' Their son-in-law Joe Coulthard with new wife and toddler were staying, and their neighbours and landlords, the delightfully named Monsieur and Madame Bonjour, joined them for part of the time.

On 1 January 1903, Hudson handed over the general directorship officially and fully to Hoste. Hudson became consulting director, stating he wished Mr Hoste always to be free to consult him. The question as to whether Mr Hoste would feel free not to was not raised. But grace undergirded this new territory for them both. By 18 February he had heard back affirmatively from all four councils on the matter. Dixon Hoste remained as general director of the China Inland Mission for a further thirty-five years.

Jennie was writing at this time of the pattern of her husband's health, feeling low, then rallying, but each time feeling he could be 'taken'. Some of this was undoubtedly a human reaction to having handed over great responsibility. In the *Monthly Notes*, the more detailed newsletter for members of CIM only, Mr Hoste updated them on his recent visits to the Taylors in Switzerland. He asked for prayer for them, still emphasising Mrs Taylor was looking after Mr Taylor. Also in the New Year they had a flying visit from Howard and Geraldine, who were about to be escorted on a tour of the Middle East. This was a gift for all their hard work in the States, with the spiritual enrichment and widening of missionary horizons that a visit to Palestine would bring.

The Taylors' new home became something of a CIM centre among the mountains. With extra rooms at the *pension*, many visitors from the UK were able to stay. Everyone was taken on daily walks. One visitor reported that the Taylors were 'rejoicing in the flowers by day, and studying the stars at night'.

22

'We Match One Another Very Well' (1903–04)

Gradually it was others who took Hudson for his walks: Jennie was finding excuses not to go. She was beginning to get very tired, and her appetite was no longer responding to the clear mountain air.

So instead, she sat by the window watching others go for walks. She was ready on their return with a tea tray, and news from the latest mail (of which there were four daily deliveries). She and Hudson continued to indulge in their love of nature, enjoying together the wild alpine flowers Hudson brought home for pressing. Botany and photography were real gifts from God at this time.

They were both looking forward to a visit from Hudson's son Charlie, but that summer he went down with pleurisy. The faithful Amy was with them, but they missed seeing their only home-based son.

Then in July 1903, Howard and Geraldine, back from the Middle East and speaking in Keswick, suddenly received an urgent telegram concerning Jennie. This was so unusual as to seem alarming: it was always Hudson who was ill.

They left straight for Switzerland – where Jennie described her symptoms to doctor son Howard. But distressingly her appearance gave away a lot also. Howard advised she see a specialist straight away. As ever, Jennie held back from making a fuss, but miraculously as it seemed to them all, a medical friend from America, a member of the CIM North American Council, just happened to be in Switzerland at a medical conference in Chamonix, hardly fifty miles away. So, Jennie submitted to being seen by him at a private hospital in Lausanne – where things seemed to start moving rather faster. An operation was planned for 15 August. Not altogether surprisingly Hudson, in a state of nervous collapse over what was happening, was too ill to be there. This was what Jennie had dreaded, far more, in fact, than actually being ill. Howard therefore stayed with his father at a hotel, while Geraldine remained at Jennie's bedside. Jennie wrote a note to Hudson while she was awaiting this new unknown. 'If only I could have spared you it all,' she wrote characteristically. 'Dear Geraldine would tell you . . . I am resting happily in the Lord.'

In fact, just a minor procedure revealed that further surgery was pointless. The senior Taylors were told surgery was not necessary, with the implication that this was good news. Did they guess? Maybe it was just the next generation who remained in ignorance, not of the diagnosis itself, but of the awareness of how much the parents knew. Jennie certainly knew she had a 'fibrous tumour', referring to it in correspondence, but not commenting on its obvious doom-laden tone. She knew it was suspected, retrospectively, that her mother had died of stomach cancer.

In letters she explained there had been the possibility of major surgery, saying her relief was far more for her husband, who had been in such a nervous state when the possibility, with all its attendant risks, was looming. Major abdominal surgery, as yet in its infancy, still held well-founded fears for its subjects. It had only been possible at all since aseptic technique along with general anaesthesia had been refined within the last ten years.

Soon it was time for Howard and Geraldine to leave again. Hudson and Jennie remained in Lausanne for the winter, taking rented rooms, with 'a treasure of a maid'. Here a doctor was on hand, also an English-speaking church. They had the whole ground floor of *Beau Reveil*, a lovely house with 'a piano and a good striking clock'. There were new electric trams gliding right past the door – 'at the garden gate', in fact.

Jennie wrote more than forty letters in the lead-up to Christmas, including one or two in French. The tram featured in most letters. It was a mercy to her, at a time when her walking ability was slowly declining, to be able to get out and about, into town or up the mountainside, so easily. In comparison, she wrote, 'I was a prisoner at Les Chevalleyres.' Hudson was not able to write any letters – 'his head will not now allow of his writing', Jennie explained to several.

All her letters included personal words of encouragement, often with a financial enclosure; it was a delight to them to be able to be generous at this stage in their lives. Much to her surprise, following legal proceedings on the residuary estate of her Australian uncle, Jennie had recently again become beneficiary of a considerable sum.

Separately, Hudson still kept abreast of CIM finances, particularly the extensive bequests, which brought so much responsibility. He enquired how many more payments were due from the estate of their yacht-dwelling businessman friend. There were also the enormous benefactions of Isabella Bird (whom the CIM persistently called Mrs Bird Bishop) and the possibility of a hospital in Honan, in memory of her father.

Incredibly even with Jennie's obvious decline, Hudson felt some comfort in being able to share his lesser ailments with her – so she often mentioned them to others: one day he suffered indigestion, which could only be put down to 'taking his porridge in bed'. And again, 'My dear husband and I have our ups and downs but are fairly well' but 'Amy is not strong'. Amy, in fact, suffered from occasional headaches 'and a lassitude that for a young girl troubles me'. Jennie sent her to a doctor; he advised her not to drink tea or coffee, which if it were migraines would possibly have been efficacious. Jennie's time was still full with caring for others.

She was also learning to pace herself. She wrote to her father about her increasing weariness (as well as everyone else's ailments), but stated that short walks were still a blessing.

Mr Faulding himself died peacefully on 25 March 1904. He had given two daughters to China – but his sons William and Alfred were both on hand at the end; Jennie was glad at least he was not around to see her weakening. Great respect was shown throughout the town on the day of the 86-year-old's funeral: the church bell tolled, shops shut and drew their blinds, and an ex-mayor of Tenterden rode with the sons and widow. And Jennie was left even better off.

In spite of being eleven years younger, Jennie was not now going to outlive her husband. Yet he himself was frail, and might die soon after. These facts being so, a solicitor friend advised them, distressing as it was at this stage, to rewrite their wills in favour of their children, rather than each other. In spite of incredible generosity, Jennie was discovering she could not outgive God; it looked as if she would die a wealthy woman.

In April they moved back to *La Paisible* in the village of Les Chevalleyres. Jennie being weaker now was less aware of being restricted. She sat on the balcony watching the birds in the cherry blossom; in the meadows beyond, the spring narcissi were just poking through. And they rejoiced also in generally good news from China.

Jennie reported she was happily still mobile, but was sometimes uncomfortable – and growing thinner. Her specialist was able to give symptomatic relief. She said Hudson was frail also – 'we match one another very well'.

In May she had a letter from Henry Frost, who expressed relief that she and Hudson were 'rather better'! But he also requested she be 'frank and honest' with him. Friends were beginning to suspect the truth. Clearly Jennie felt relief at being honest, and another letter from Mr Frost on 14 July indicated he had most definitely been told. From June onwards Jennie had started telling people she knew she was 'on her way home', perhaps within a few days.

Geraldine was speaking at Keswick in the summer of 1904, but Howard with Amelia Broomhall came to stay on 7 June; he noticed the deterioration in Jennie, who was now only managing liquids. To Jennie his arrival was a relief, as she felt he could take over 'managing' his father. Amy was picking up on the increasing nursing duties.

Jennie's letters were getting shorter, but an oft-repeated theme was of being spoilt, and aware now she was spared life's everyday trials. But news from China was still encouraging her heart.

On 24 June she wrote 'my strength seems ebbing fast away'. She was emphatic about not wanting to linger on in helplessness. By the end of June, she was sparing herself the effort of dressing every day; this, she said, conserved her energy. With French windows open onto fresh air and the outside world, and the doors behind her onto the living room, she felt connected with everyone and everything. Her spirit was still buoyant: 'I could not be better cared for or happier.' The young-at-heart, generous-spirited Jennie still won through.

Then Hudson's son Charles, much to his father's delight, came to stay for a fortnight. Charles had no memory of his mother, Maria – indeed, as a toddler he had not recognised his father when Hudson came to collect him from Ningpo for their journey home from China. On that voyage he became acquainted with both his father and the fiancée, Miss Faulding, for the first time. On arrival home he had the advantage over his siblings, who still had to adjust to the new family dynamic. Now he had come to Switzerland to say goodbye to the one who had truly been his mother. As he stooped over her to kiss her, she reached out with her thin arms, wrapping them around him, her son whom she loved as much as any of them, and to whom she'd grown close in those years when his father and three older siblings had been in China. He had shared his hurts and frustrations with her. He had no sense with Jennie he had let her down.

'We Match One Another Very Well' (1903–04)   253

Later he wrote a letter; it was practical rather than emotional. It had been important to him, while he was staying there, that as a caring son he had thanked the Bonjours for everything; now it was important to him that he shared this with his parents.

The Bonjours had a chambermaid who spoke English and was a trained nurse. They put her at Jennie's disposal, and if there were any night-time requirements she could have her, they said, and they would find another. Howard had thought there might be weeks of distress at the end, with vomiting perhaps, and even fluids not tolerated, but so far this was not so.

At Keswick, Geraldine received a letter. In it, Jennie spoke of the 'sweet power of helplessness'. She said she would like to see Geraldine if possible, but was praying for her 'among the thronging multitudes'. She said she was living now just from day to day. Unknowingly, she had just two weeks to go. Geraldine set out as soon as she could be free from her Keswick responsibilities.

On 29 July, Jennie struggled to dictate goodbye letters to close friends and family. She was still enquiring about others. Too weak now to say much, at midday she slowly managed 'my love to Geraldine if she isn't in time'.

'I'm nearly Home' she whispered slowly on the same day. 'What will it be to be there?' She was now on the very doorstep of heaven. She had completed the difficult part, and all she wanted to do was sleep – the sooner to wake in Paradise, with her Saviour's arms securely around her. An hour later she asked if there was any word from Ernest.

On the whole, she had been spared suffering; almost her final words were uttered to assure those around her she was not in pain. Then her breathing became distressed during the night; she cried out a couple of times in the last hour or so, finally asking Hudson to pray that she would be 'taken'.

At 8 o'clock on the morning of Saturday 30 July 1904, her breathing changed; no longer struggling she slipped into unconsciousness: her journey was probably already over. She died at six minutes past eight, with Hudson, Amy and Howard at her side. She was not quite 61.

A telegram was sent immediately to Newington Green. The news reached Theodore Howard, and he wrote to Hudson the same day. His letter was answered by Geraldine, to save her distraught father-in-law. The detail she supplied therein formed the basis of her *In Memoriam*, the little pocket-sized booklet she wrote as a tribute to Jennie.

A week later, a brief funeral service was held in the house, following which Howard and the Swiss pastor walked ahead of the cortege the two miles to the Swiss Reformed Church in the village of St Légier-La Chiésaz, where a quiet spot had been chosen in the graveyard. Geraldine and Amy took a carriage with Hudson. A folding chair was brought along to enable him to sit by the graveside for the second service, which was in French and English. Locals joined them from the village, together with friends from Vevey, down by the lake. And their friends the Count and Countess from Blonay were there. Hudson, deeply distressed, nevertheless shook hands with all who had gathered.

Jennie's grave, piled high with flowers for many weeks, was a favourite quiet place for Hudson. There was even a seat under the spread of a nearby cedar. Anyone standing there would see the woods and fields behind the church, and in front a magnificent vista of the lake, with the towering French Alps beyond.

Postscript

Hudson remained in *La Paisible* until after the winter. Early in 1905 he felt stronger, and started expressing a wish to see China once more. So, travelling via North America, Howard and Geraldine took him back for a final visit. They reached Changsha in Hunan province – and here Hudson died suddenly and peacefully on 3 June. He was buried next to his first wife, Maria. He had been spared the anniversary of Jennie's death.

Sadly in a way, Jennie had no grandchildren of her own.

Ernest married Elsie Gauntlett in October 1907 – but she was already 38, six years older than Ernest. She had arrived in China in 1896, and had survived the horrors of the Boxer Rebellion. They had a long life together of useful service.

Amy returned to London, and studied for a while at the Highbury Athenaeum. For some years she lived at Newington Green with her cousin Marshall Broomhall and his wife, Florence, helping them with their children. She was described as a gentle, affectionate and somewhat devout soul, with a penchant in later life for the High Church.

In the Second World War, it had been recommended that those not immediately involved in the war effort should move out of London. Howard felt responsible for his never-married half-sister, so now in her sixties she moved from Newington Green to live near Howard and Geraldine, when they eventually retired to the UK, settling in Southborough near Tunbridge Wells, Kent. It was said she had the 'Taylor affliction' – both she and Howard were prematurely deaf.

Then three years into the war, Amy moved to Hertfordshire to look after Ernest, back from China after losing Elsie in 1942.

Amy and Geraldine remained close, corresponding to the end of Geraldine's life.

Along with their two older half-brothers, Herbert and Howard, Ernest and Amy both lived until after the Second World War. They are both buried in Tunbridge Wells Cemetery, in the 'CIM corner'.

And Charles? He was the only Taylor son around when Amelia Broomhall died in 1918; so along with four Broomhall sons and one grandson, he helped carry the coffin of his aunt, neighbour and sometime surrogate mother.

It would have gratified Jennie to know he remained an honoured member of the extended family.

Appendix 1

Hudson Taylor's surviving children

With Maria:
1861 Herbert Hudson born, April
1862 Frederick Howard born, November
1867 Maria Hudson born, February
1868 Charles Edward born, November

With Jennie:
1875 Ernest Hamilton born, January
1876 Amy Hudson born, April
1877 Mary Jane 'Millie' Duncan 'adopted' (born 1870 approx.)

1881 Herbert **to China** aged 20
1884 Maria **to China** aged 17
1886 Herbert married aged 25
1888 Maria married aged 21
1888 Howard **to China** aged 26
1894 Howard married aged 31
1898 Ernest **to China** aged 23
1907 Ernest married aged 32

Appendix 2

Summary of Jennie's six journeys to China

1866–71 – as Miss Faulding, with the *Lammermuir* party.

1872–74 – as Mrs Taylor, with her husband.

1878–81 – with a party of women to the Shansi famine; later joined by Hudson.

(Hudson Taylor travels to China three times without Jennie)

1890–92 – travelling alone; joins Hudson in China; return via Canada (circumnavigating the globe, crossing Dateline in easterly direction).

1894–96 – travelling with Hudson, and Geraldine Guinness, via America; visit to India before return (circumnavigating the globe, crossing Dateline in westerly direction).

1897–99 – travelling with Hudson, and Henrietta Soltau, via America, returning via Australia, New Zealand, and America again, thus crossing Dateline twice.

Bibliography

Aitchison, Margaret. *The Doctor and the Dragon* (Basingstoke: Pickering & Inglis, 1983).

Bacon, Daniel W. *From Faith to Faith* (Singapore: Overseas Missionary Fellowship (IHQ) Ltd, 1984).

Barber, W.T.A. *David Hill: Missionary and Saint* (London: Charles H. Kelly, 1903).

Barr, Pat. *To China with Love* (London: Secker & Warburg, 1972).

Bird, Isabella. *The Yangtze Valley and Beyond* (London: Virago, 1985).

Broomhall, A.J. *Hudson Taylor and China's Open Century, Books I-VII* (Sevenoaks: Hodder & Stoughton, 1989).

*Broomhall, B. *The Evangelisation of the World: A Missionary Band, a Record of Consecration and an Appeal* (London: Morgan & Scott, 1887).

Broomhall, Marshall. *The Jubilee Story of the China Inland Mission* (London: Morgan & Scott Ltd, 1915).

Broomhall, Ruth. *Called by God into the Heart of the Dragon* (Farnham: CWR, 2018).

Cable, Mildred and Francesca French. *A Woman Who Laughed* (London: The China Inland Mission, 1934).

Cable, Mildred and Francesca French. *China: Her Life and Her People* (London: University of London Press, 1946).

Chang, Jung. *Wild Swans* (London: Flamingo, 1993).

Cliff, Norman. *A Flame of Sacred Love* (Carlisle: OM Publishing, 1998).

Cook, Faith. *Troubled Journey* (Edinburgh: Banner of Truth Trust, 2004).

Cox, Jessica. *Confinement: The Hidden History of Maternal Bodies in Nineteenth-Century Britain* (Cheltenham: The History Press, 2023).

Cronin, A.J. *The Keys of the Kingdom* (Sevenoaks: Hodder & Stoughton, 1988).

Fleming, Peter. *News from Tartary* (London: Jonathan Cape, 1936).

Foxell, Simon. *Mapping London* (London: Black Dog Publishing, 2007).

Griffiths, Valerie. *Not Less Than Everything* (Oxford: Monarch, 2004).

Guinness, Joy. *Mrs Howard Taylor: Her Web of Time* (London: China Inland Mission, 1949).

Guinness, Michele. *The Guinness Spirit* (London: Hodder & Stoughton, 2000).

Hill-Murphy, Jacki. *The Life and Travels of Isabella Bird* (Yorkshire: Pen & Sword, 2021).

Houghton, Frank. *China Calling* (London: China Inland Mission, 1948).

Jones, Edward and Christopher Woodward. *Guide to the Architecture of London* (London: Phoenix, 2013).

Martin, Gordon. *Chefoo School 1881–1951* (Braunton, Devon: Merlin Books Ltd, 1990).

Pollock, John. *Hudson Taylor and Maria* (Eastbourne: Kingsway, 1983).

Pollock, John. *The Cambridge Seven* (Basingstoke: Marshall, Morgan & Scott, 1985).

Reeve, Rev B. *Timothy Richard DD, China Missionary, Statesman & Reformer* (London: S.W. Partridge & Co Ltd, 1910).

Steer, Roger. *J. Hudson Taylor: A Man in Christ* (Carlisle: OMF & Paternoster Lifestyle, 2001).

Taylor, Dr and Mrs Howard. *The Growth of a Work of God* (London: China Inland Mission & Religious Tract Society, 1925).

Taylor, Dr and Mrs Howard. *'By Faith' – Henry W. Frost and the China Inland Mission* (Philadelphia, PA: CIM, 1938).

Taylor, Mrs Howard. *In Memoriam: Mrs Hudson Taylor* (undated, unpublished printed booklet).

*Taylor, J. Hudson. *China's Spiritual Need and Claims* (London: Morgan & Scott, 1884).

Thompson, Phyllis. *D.E. Hoste: A Prince with God* (London: CIM, 1947).

Thompson, Phyllis. *Each to Her Post* (Sevenoaks: Hodder & Stoughton, 1882).

Thompson, Phyllis. *No Bronze Statue* (London: Word Books, 1972).

Thompson, Wardlaw. *Griffith John* (London: Religious Tract Society, 1906).

Time-Life editors. *China* (Amsterdam: Time-Life, 1984).

Tomalin, Claire. *The Life and Death of Mary Wollstonecraft* (London: Penguin, 2012).

Trevelyan, G.M. *English Social History* (London: Longman, Green and Co., 1945).

Weightman, Gavin, and Steve Humphries. *The Making of Modern London 1815–1914* (London: Sidgwick & Jackson, 1983).

Wheeler, Harold (general editor). *The Wonderful Story of London* (London: Odhams Press Ltd, 1937).

Wigram, Christopher E.M. *The Bible and Mission in Faith Perspective* (Zoetermeer: Boekencentrum, 2007).

Yen Mah, Adeline. *Falling Leaves* (London: Penguin, 1997).

*Title of book has changed slightly from original publication

From a background in nursing, and in church ministry alongside her husband, Marion Osgood is now archivist for OMF International (UK), as well as leading local guided walks, and working with Foodbank. Marion has travelled widely, particularly within the developing world, fulfilling a variety of engagements and roles. She and her husband live in Bromley, UK. For relaxation they enjoy country walking, and visiting their children and grandchildren, both locally and in beautiful parts of the north of England.

Jennie Hudson Taylor is Marion's third published biography, the others being *Whatever Happened to Kathy Keay?* (2010) and *Call the Desert Midwife* (2021).

For more information visit: www.marionosgood.com

We hope you enjoyed the story of God's faithfulness through the life of Jennie Taylor.

Jennie served with the China Inland Mission, which was founded by James Hudson Taylor in 1865 and continues to proclaim the gospel today as OMF International.

We serve the Church and share the good news of Jesus Christ in all its fullness in countries across East Asia. We're for all Christians who want to be relevant in mission. We're a forward-thinking gospel-focused movement that pursues every avenue to reach East Asians for Jesus. In a changing world, we need to find the most effective means possible.

Today this looks like around 1,400 workers from 40 countries serving across East Asia. Their ministries vary from church planting to medical work, from sport to theological education. Each of them seeks to serve the Church and share the good news of Jesus Christ.

*Discover more about OMF, our work in East Asia and find free resources at **omf.org***

Heart for Asia. Hope for Billions.

/omfinternational   omf_int   omf_int

Authentic

We trust you enjoyed reading this book from Authentic. If you want to be informed of any new titles from this author and other releases you can sign up to the Authentic newsletter by scanning below:

Online:
authenticmedia.co.uk

Follow us:

www.ingramcontent.com/pod-product-compliance
Ingram Content Group UK Ltd.
Pitfield, Milton Keynes, MK11 3LW, UK
UKHW022016200825
462079UK00005B/27

9 781788 933414